Manuscript for

NON-FICTION BOOK

AN END TO IMMIGRATION

Sunil Sharan

Sunil Sharan
3572 Sunnyhaven Dr
San Jose, CA 95117, USA
sunil.sharan22@gmail.com

Contents

1. Immigration to the US from Europe and now India

Immigration to countries and land masses has been happening since time immemorial. Rarely has a large influx of people been peaceful, and rarely has it been good for the incumbent population. One need only look at what the Conquistadors did in South America. Closer home we have the American example.

By one account, Native Americans gave the European foreigners corn and other food. The white foreigners attacked them instead, and celebrate their victory as Thanksgiving. I would say that no good came out of white immigration to America for the native population. Today the natives are consigned to reservations, which have become dens for gambling, drugs and drink.

Except for certain areas like New Mexico, one seldom sees an American Indian out in the open. They are a broken lot. Treaty after treaty that they signed with the white man was violated by the latter. They were left with no recourse because the white man was more powerful, ruthless and merciless. In California, I saw a beautiful bumper sticker on a car being driven by a Native American. It said, Love America or Give It Back.

It is a question mark though whether the white man has loved America. Maybe a lot? Or just a wee little bit? Certainly the Native Americans lived off the land and preserved the pristine shape of the country. The white man brought guns, alcohol and drugs, and disease (very often venereal disease) and decimated the Native American populations with them.

The objective here is not to hold anyone accountable. Men have wrought uncountable miseries on other men. It is just to exemplify what happens to an incumbent population when a strange population makes rapid ingress. Incumbent men and women are often targeted. Places of worship are brought down in haste. Foreign religions are imposed. Actually a whole new way of life takes over.

The white man settled the land, as if the land was unsettled before he came over. But still, the settlement went ahead as he knew it, as per European procedure. Wave upon wave of different kinds of Europeans landed on America's shores. The English, the German, the Scotch-Irish, the Jew, followed by the Italian and the Irish. It took some time for the Northern and Western Europeans to accept the Southern Europeans like the Italian as white.

But despite personal reservations, intermingling happened. I asked an American woman what her heritage was, and she said that I am just a European mutt. The whites of course imported the blacks from Africa and the Chinese for their railroads, and went about building America. Skyscrapers dotted the skylines of major American cities. Do you know who built these skyscrapers? It was the Canadian Indians, for they have no fear of heights.

In the 1600s, a forced migration of people began from Africa to America called the slave trade. During the Jim Crow years, which followed the end of the American Civil War, a new slogan, "separate but equal" cropped up to justify segregation and racial discrimination. Separate but equal meant that whites and blacks led separate but equal lives. Yes, their lives were separate, but very unequal. Racial integration was encouraged after Jim Crow but that only served to consign blacks to downtown ghettos and a flight of whites from downtown to the suburbs.

Today, by law racial discrimination is banned but the two races—white and black—still don't mix. Blacks constitute about 15% of the population, but even after the civil rights movement and the election of the first black president—Barack Obama—racial disparity and friction abound. The rift between black and white seems to be eternal and is one of the major faultlines of the nation. This is another example of how forced immigration of blacks has harmed the nation.

Around the sixties, America started opening itself up to the voluntary migration of people of color. I really don't know what the motivation was. Perhaps it was altruistic, to allow a few people from the Third World to share in the prosperity of America. Perhaps there was a labor shortage. Around the same time, major English universities like Oxford and Cambridge shut their doors to foreign students by denying them scholarships. Major US universities, flush with cash from endowments and inventions, welcomed bright Third World citizens with open arms and financial aid.

Before independence from the British in 1947 and for a couple of decades afterwards, Indian students went to England for studies. But with the abolishment of scholarships and with them being found in plenty in the US, they diverted themselves to the latter. Still it was only a trickle.

My older brother took off for the States in 1984, my older sister in 1986, and I followed in 1990. I left many wonderful opportunities in India behind to pursue a PhD at Purdue University. I was all of 21. My parents didn't want me to go. I was their only remaining child in India. My father and mother sat me down on the sofa in our living room. My father was a retired army officer, and very British in his upbringing. He said that we Indians might think whatever of ourselves, but for the white man, we were just blackies.

My mother echoed his sentiments. She belonged to a small town called Jalandhar in the state of Punjab. She said that during World War II, the Tommies (as British soldiers were called then in India) stationed in her town used to sexually harass Indian women. But all of my parents' entreaties had no effect on me. My mind was made up. I wanted to see the world.

Even as late as 1990, there were not many Indian students in as prized a university as Purdue. In my department, electrical engineering, the flagship department of the university, there were not more than two or three. There was but one Indian professor.

Other departments had the same story to tell. In a university of 40,000 students, there were only about a hundred Indian students.

I know because I asked the head of the Indian Student Association. The vast majority of the students were graduate students on teaching or research assistantships, for which one had to work to get a tuition waiver and a small living stipend that took care of one's food, accommodation, and sundry other expenses.

I befriended the only Indian undergrad in the whole university. His father was a doctor in Bahrain and he was paying his way through. He was all of 16. Those days, the US Embassy in Delhi used to advise Indian undergrad students not to travel to the US to study. They said that the culture shock would be too great for a teenager. Indian parents took that piece of advice literally. Plus, most Indians, even the rich ones, could not afford paying the bills of a US university.

So the only Indians who came to the US were grad students on fellowships (which were almost impossible to get) and assistantships (which were almost as impossible to get too).

India liberalized its economy in 1991, creating a new rich class that could virtually buy anything and pay for virtually anything. India's elite engineering and medical schools were few and far between and almost impossible to gain admission into with the competition being so fierce. Even humanities and liberal arts schools had stringent standards of admission. Children of the new rich were often spoiled and did not study hard. They knew that dad had the dough to send them to undergrad school in the US.

Getting into school in the US was relatively much easier than getting into school in India. So the Indian rich kids spurned the Indian option altogether and concentrated their energies on the US. The money involved for an international student was about $50,000 a year. (I am assuming that international students pay out-of-state tuition and not more.) Many of these rich kids promised their parents that they would be back once their American studies were complete, but as soon as they landed on US shores, they had a change of heart.

My roommate at Purdue was an Indian called Rajesh. He too, like me, was a grad student, having done his undergrad studies in India. Rajesh joked that the expectation of an average Indian student was to disembark from a Lufthansa flight in the US and walk into a white woman's vagina. It was another thing that hardly any white woman gave any Indian a second glance. This was a source of much depression among the Indians. Some would frantically call home, asking to return home. I know of one case where the Indian student fled back home.

But for most Indian students, it was as if they had entered heaven from hell. India's infrastructure was (and still is) ghastly when compared to America's. Everything was spic and span in the US. Heck, even the people (not the blacks though) looked clean. The girls were fair, thereby pretty, and seemingly friendly (if you could catch them in a particular setting). Within a few days, the Indian's mind was made up. He was not returning to the shithole country that was India.

He would constantly tell his mama-papa otherwise, that he would return to India once his studies were up. Even when he returned to India on vacation, he mouthed the same mantra. But when the time came, it found him looking for a job in the US. Only the truly rich, whose dads had built empires in India would consider going back. One out of a hundred would have snagged a white girlfriend. Then there was no going back.

Stiffed was the upper middle-class parent who has exhausted all his savings in putting through his ward through an American school. He could remain stiffed or he could ask his ward to compensate for his expenses. The only way the ward could do that was by getting an American job. But it would be years before any job would pay for what the dad had spent. Still it was the worth the effort if the son worked for some years and paid the dad at least something.

But the upper middle-class Indians would still not return to India. Dad might have a factory or two in India, but life was much comfortable and convenient in the States. It had taken his dad working his entire life to put the son through school in the US. It would take him, the son, just a few years to do the same for his future son and daughter. India was a grind. Everyone knew that. Why go through it when you could have an easy life in the States.

Children of the middle and poor classes had no recourse to turn to their parents for money for their parents had no money to spare. It was here that Indian banks and foreign banks in India got into the act. They realized that one profitable investment could be investing in poor Indian students wanting to make their way to the US. They would loan them their tuition and living expenses and expect to be repaid with interest after a certain number of years.

In return, they would keep the students' parents' house as collateral, just in case the son or daughter reneged on paying their loan. This was a sweet deal for the banks. Investments as safe as this were hard to get. When I was growing in India in the eighties, a popular phrase to denote the outflux of Indian students to the US was brain drain. The prime minister of India then was Indira Gandhi. Her key advisor was a gentleman called Abid Hussain.

During a speech, Hussain was asked about the danger that brain drain posed to India. Wasn't a poor country like India subsidizing a rich country like the US through brain drain? Hussain responded that it was better for the brain to drain than to be in the drain. Gandhi was sitting on the podium, listening. She smiled, wryly. So since the early beginnings the Indian government had made no effort to curb brain drain. In fact, it had actively encouraged it.

The Indian government actually encourages the outflow of young Indians from India, all the while mouthing that they are against brain drain. In the US, you have what is called the H-1B visa, which is a work visa issued by a company to a foreign employee. Sixty-five thousand H-1B work visas is the cap every year for all countries. That means 65,000 foreign H-1B workers are let in to the US every year. Many make the transition from the work visa to permanent residence (the coveted green card).

But some people lost their jobs while on the H-1B. These people had a 10-day grace period to find another job and get on another H-1B, or else leave the country. The government of the Indian Prime Minister Narendra Modi lobbied hard with the Biden administration to extend the grace period if an H-1B employee loses her job. Now that grace period has been extended to 60 days. All the while the unemployed person has to look for a new job. The extension in the grace period is a real boon for H-1B employees as it allows them to stay in the US and find a job much more comfortably than during the previous 10-day grace period.

But it also means that more H-1B foreigners will stay on in the US and many more will be in a better position to get a green card, that is to fully immigrate to the US. Let's do a little math here. Assume that earlier, about half the 65,000 H-1B workers lost their jobs. Few found a new job in 10 days, so 30,000 returned to their home country. Now, in 60 days, 30,000 of the displaced half found a new job and only a few returned to their home country. Out of these 30,000, 25,000 became permanent residents. So in the current scenario, the US adds 25,000 new immigrants every year just from the H-1B program.

The H-1B path is not the only way to immigrate to the US from India. You can seek asylum, and apply for an immigrant visa either on your own or through chain migration, which is migration through your family network. Most of the Indian cabbies that you see in the US, or the people working in convenience stores like 7-11 have either got into the US by chain migration or by seeking asylum. In 1990, the population of people of Indian origin (PIOs) in the US was around 1 million. Today, the population of PIOs has ballooned to more than 4 million. A PIO is anyone who has Indian blood in them.

Such a rapid growth of ethnic population is causing heartburn among many other ethnicities in the US, that 4 million people are doing so well in that Indians constitute the most prosperous minority in the US, with an average income higher than that of whites or even Jews. The heartburn is so strong that every other month, an Indian or two is shot dead by thugs in the US. The Indian community turns a blind eye. They don't want anything to disturb their peace and tranquility.

The Modi government, so vocal on so many international issues, too keeps mum. Healthy remittances flow into the coffers of the government from Indians settled in America. A few Indians killed every year are just collateral damage to the fantastic success story of the Indian diaspora in America. A Sundar Pichai (CEO of Google) or a Satya Nadella (CEO of Microsoft) are felicitated regularly by the government and people of India, in fact they have become household names in India, but everyone is deathly quiet about the murder of a poor H-1B worker.

One would expect that at least a Pichai or a Nadella, secure in the foolproof bodily security that their companies provide them, would say something, but there is nary a peep from any of them. They are American citizens now and must not look parochial in taking cudgels on behalf of people of their former nationality. With their American nationality, they also shed their Indian, just as so many reptiles shed their old skin for the new. India, in any case, does not allow dual nationality. If you gain some other country's, you must renounce the Indian.

Just recently, I had a gun pointed at my face. It was a blood-curling experience. I had made an unexpected turn, which bothered the car behind. I corrected course immediately, but the other car started stalking me. I tried to shake him off but couldn't.

He pulled up beside me and lo and behold, waived a gun right in my face. He looked Punjabi (from the Indian state of Punjab). My life was dangling by a thread. I knew that I had to get him to talk.

I asked him if he was Punjabi. He replied gruffly, no, Mexican. Many Punjabis resemble Mexicans. All I could blurt out was I love Mexico (which in fact I do), I love Mexican people. He lowered his gun and told me to scram. I took off like I had seen a ghost. I had to, because my life depended upon it.

I had faced guns before. Once, in college at Urbana-Champaign, Illinois, a hooded man had entered a Taco Bell where I was eating. He ordered everyone to lie flat on the floor, and went up to the cashier. Mercifully, he didn't come to any of the diners. He collected his loot and disappeared on a bike. My right leg started shaking out of fear. Soon enough there were about 10 cop cars surrounding the restaurant.

Once at a cruise ship terminal in Mumbai, India, I had a security guard point his assault rifle at my chin. But, strangely enough, I felt no fear then. With the Mexican, it was different. I was deathly afraid. I had heard about Mexican gangs and cartels in the US. But I had never ever encountered a violent Mexican. Now I realized that the danger from some Mexican immigrants was real. They act as if they are in Mexico, with the same brazenness, with the same mercilessness. I didn't want to be added to the nameless list of silent deaths that so many of my Indian brothers had got affixed to.

Now wherever I go in the US, I always watch my back. I know resentment against Indians is high. But it was bound to be, and if Indian immigration continues like this, the resentment will only increase. Today every upper- and middle-class home in India has someone settled in the US. When I was young, I applied for a tourist US visa at the US embassy in New Delhi. Both my older brother and older sister were in the States. I was the youngest of three siblings. The consular officer at the embassy refused my visa.

He said that it was apparent that parental responsibility ran deeply in my family. (My parents would be left alone in India were I too to also leave for the US.) That taunt cut deep. Worse was when I got out of the embassy. My dad was waiting outside. I told him I had been rejected. Dejected, he responded that he had never failed an interview in his life. That hurt even more.

The concept of old-age homes did not exist in India until the eighties. These were supposed to exist purely in the West, and were in fact seen as one of the many maladies of western culture. To abandon old parents in India was a sin. There is a story of a Hindu boy called Shravan Kumar who used to carry his parents on his back. One was supposed to even forsake marriage and kids to look after old parents. I am single without issue and have dedicated my life to my parents.

There is no greater satisfaction. When my father died, I promised myself that my mom would not die alone. So I returned to India from the US. Many people are stunned that I have given up "USA life" for my mom, but there it is. I feel awkward in India. I have been out 28 years and know no one. Since I am only a struggling writer, no one wants to know me either. It's a tough, lonely life, but I have the satisfaction of taking care of my mom. India is truly the wild, wild east.

Now so many Indians who have left for the US have parents who cannot stomach the life there. They suffer from the same sickness—loneliness—in the US that I do in India. So, many old-age homes have sprouted up all over India. They are all bursting at the seams. At one of the most prestigious clubs in India, the Delhi Golf Club, there are massive hoardings everywhere advertising old-age homes, with all kinds of amenities and facilities for the elderly.

The golf club's clientele is mainly old Indian males, many of them having wards in the US, with no hope of their coming back. The golfer is still sprightly, but he knows that in a few years, he will need care. Hence the hoardings to attract him. Living alone in India is not safe for a couple. My mother had two robberies, with all her jewelry stolen. Many Indians have help—part-time or full-time—and very often they commit or connive in the thefts. The police typically end up doing nothing.

Some parents do elect to move to the US with their children. I used to live in Atlanta. I called in AT&T's technician to fix my internet router. A short, middle-aged, seemingly white woman rang my bell. We got talking. She said that she was not white, but fully Native American. She confided that she faced a lot of discrimination on the job, especially from old white ladies who didn't want to have anything to do with her. They would throw her out of the house the minute they realized that she not white but Native American.

I shared my stories of discrimination with her. She responded that I was a single, colored male who mixed and mingled with the locals, so I was bound to get the short end of the stick. She sad that many Indian houses that she visited had a couple, their parents, and their children. They never associated with anyone. Every evening, the whole family would go for a walk, talk to no one, and return home. These people never encountered any discrimination because they kept so close to themselves.

Old-age homes, nursing homes, loneliness (for both parents in India and in the US), these are just some of the ill-effects of unabated emigration from India to the US. Many of the young who migrate totally blank out their parents and their plight from their minds, except perhaps for a weekly check-in call. They want to date, marry, have children, get on with their lives, pretending as if their parents do not exist. Very often the parents find matches for them in India, after which they tell their parents to get lost. We have no room for you.

One of my college mates went to the US and founded a company. He sold it, making some money in the process. I met him when I was in the States. Both of his kids were about to graduate from college. He emphasized how important the future of his kids was to him. His father was a retired three-star general of the Indian army. As I recollect it, both of his parents were 85 years old. They were visiting him from India.

My friend said that this would be the last time they would be making the trek from India to the US. With great difficulty, they had managed to make that journey this time. Since he had already come into some money, I asked why doesn't he and his wife move back to India for a few years to look after his parents. He dismissed my suggestion offhand. He said that his kids were much more important to him than his parents. Another elderly couple going the way of living alone or the old-age home, I guess. I was speaking to another friend about this and she said that I didn't realize how visceral a bond there is between parents and their kids. I have no kids, so I wouldn't know. I only have my mom, and earlier my dad, and know how visceral a bond I shared with my father, and now share with my mother.

2. What immigration has done to India

India has had a glorious past, not just over the last 5,000 years but perhaps even much longer. The Indus Valley Civilization of the third millennium BCE is one of the first recorded human civilizations anywhere in the world. It was centered around the River Indus, now in Pakistan. North India gave rise to the flourishing Maurya and Gupta Empires, which soon spread to the rest of the subcontinent.

Under the Mauryas, internal and external trade, agriculture, and economic activities thrived and expanded across South Asia due to the creation of a single and efficient system of finance, administration, and security. Emperor Ashoka, who ruled from 268–232 BCE, was one of the most prominent rulers of the Maurya Dynasty. He fought the Kalinga War, and after beholding the ensuing bloodshed, embraced Buddhism and sent Buddhist missionaries to Sri Lanka, Northwest India, and South East Asia.

Ashoka occupies a singular status in India today. It is his seal that is the country's official seal. The statuettes of his lions adorn the Indian Parliament. His conversion to Buddhism reflects India's secularism. For the first time in the history of the country, a ruler had embraced another faith but was still adored by his people, who remained Hindu for the most part. India's population during his time is estimated to have been between 15 and 30 million.

The Gupta Empire followed and existed between the 3rd century CE and the mid-6th century CE. At its zenith, it covered much of the Indian Subcontinent. Its rule has been described as the golden age of India. Its high points were the great cultural developments that took place during its time. Many Hindu epics were canonized during this period.

The Gupta era produced scholars such as Kalidasa, Aryabhata, Varahamihira, and Vatsyayana, who made great advancements in different academic fields.

The period, sometimes described as *Pax Gupta*, gave rise to achievements in architecture, sculpture, and painting that set standards of form and taste that determined the whole subsequent course of art, not only in India but far beyond its borders.

The above recounting is not so much as to display India's splendid past, but it is to prove the naysayers, like the British, wrong when they claim that India was not a nation before they came and that they were the first ones to unite India into an administratively governable whole.

The prophet of Islam died in 632 CE. Soon thereafter, Arabic armies set out from Arabia to spread the faith in other countries. Their first target was Persia. After converting the whole of Persia to Islam, they made their way to Central Asia. But these were barren lands. The Arabs had traded for millennia, well before Muhammad emerged on the scene, with Hind (India). They knew what Hind had to offer.

In the early seven hundreds, the Arabs launched their invasion of India. They were led by a 13-year old general called Muhammad bin Qasim, who conquered the western Indian province of Sindh (now in Pakistan).

He made the whole province Islamic by defeating Sindh's Hindu ruler, Raja Dheer. Dheer is remembered in folk ballads in Singh even until today for he was considered a kind and just ruler. So began the Islamic immigration into India. It was not the first large-scale invasion of India, but previous invaders had miscegenated with the locals and co-opted themselves into the Hindu faith and culture. So, Indians today consider the Islamic invasion as the first large-scale immigration because it came with a foreign faith, as well as mass looting and pillaging.

Islam was a radically different faith from Hinduism. Islam forbade idolatory. In fact, the prophet of Islam broke many idols of ancient Arabic gods when he introduced his new faith in Mecca. Hinduism is a religion based on idolatory. When asked by Emperor Akbar (the only Muslim ruler Hindus hold in high esteem for he didn't break their temples and he let them freely practice their faith) why Hindus need idols to pray, Hindu priests replied that it helps concentrate their minds.

Other differences in practice are myriad and immutable. Muslims circumcise, even their baby girls, Hindus abhor the practice. Muslims eat meat, with a big emphasis on beef. Eating meat is forbidden in Hinduism. Many Hindus consume meat nevertheless, but refrain from touching beef. A Muslim man can have four wives simultaneously, Hindus only one, although it must be said that in years before independence from the British in 1947, Hindus too freely practiced polygamy.

Muslims bury their dead; Hindus cremate. Muslims, especially their men, can divorce easily, Hindus not so. Hindus believe a marriage lasts for seven lifetimes (Hindus believe in reincarnation). Muslims proselytize, in fact spreading the faith is the foundational principle of Islam; Hindus do not convert as a rule. So the differences between Islam and Hinduism are vast, amounting to a chasm. When the Islamic immigrants came to India, they were met with disdain.

The period from Qasim's conquest of Sindh to the end of the twelfth century are almost five hundred years—virtually half a millennium—but they are hazy in Indian history.

What is certain is that many Arabic and Central Asian Muslim raiders came to India but they were thwarted by local Hindu rulers. A seminal event occurred in 1191 CE. Prithviraj Chauhan was a Hindu king who ruled over a large swathe of northern India, including Delhi, from his capital in Ajmer, in the present-day Indian state of Rajasthan. Muhammed Ghori from Ghor in present-day Afghanistan invaded India.

Chauhan defeated him in battle. The following year Ghori reemerged with reinforcements and vanquished Chauhan. Chauhan was the last Hindu ruler of India for another 750 years, when the British left India.

Chauhan could have easily decapitated Ghor when he defeated him in 1191 CE. But he was magnanimous and let him go. This is what happens when an indigenous population is kind to forced immigration. The invaders do not give up; in fact, they bay for revenge. Ghor laid the foundations of Islamic rule in South Asia, which lasted after him uninterruptedly for more than half a millennium under evolving Muslim dynasties.

Often two Hindu princes would be feuding, and one would invite a Muslim foreign king to invade India and fight on his behalf. There were many a Hindu prince, so many a local feud, hence many a Muslim invader. But the Muslim invader was not interested in settling any feud. He first devoured the second Hindu king, then the one who had invited him in the first place, and then raped and pillaged at will.

This is what occurs, whether under forced immigration like an invasion, or with immigrants chosen by the indigenous population. When it comes to immigrating, immigrants are on their knees, begging to be let in. But once they are ensconced in a place, they start finding faults with it, and want to change it to their whims and fancies.

There must be some reason immigrants see attraction in a new place. It could be money or the comeliness of its women. But once they have secured a sinecure, their past starts haunting them.

They become rosy-eyed and tear-filled about the places they emigrated from. They want to emulate their old practices in their new lands. Consider dress. In Muslim states women wear the full-faced burqa. I believe that it is ordained in the Koran that a woman will not show her face and body to strange men, only to men of her immediate household. Thus the burqa was devised. I am sure that when Qasim came to India, Indian women wore the sari and other dresses, they might even have covered their heads, but few (a substantial few though) covered their faces in front of strange men.

But there was a large chunk of women who did not cover their face. In Islamic rule under him in Sindh, most women must have converted to Islam and worn the fully-veiled burqa. But what about the rest of women who remained Hindu. They lived in dread that they would be converted to Islam and then have to be fully veiled in public.

The veil has had wild ramifications in modern India. I live in a neighborhood with a number of Muslims. Most of the Muslim women, without fail, wear the burqa. I met the governor of the Indian state of Rajasthan at a function. He is Muslim. In India today, there is a raging debate over what is called love-jihad, which is that Muslim men are waging a jihad to lure Hindu women. I asked the governor about it. He said that he had a Hindu girlfriend. He went on to say that Hindu women are very gregarious, they go to parties and all that, and Muslim men find that aspect of theirs very attractive. Muslim women on the other hand typically stay at home and therefore lose their charm for many Muslim men.

But many Muslim women are quite striking. Hindu men would also like to have the chance to betroth them. But how can you fall in love with someone you cannot see, someone who flaps their bodies inside a tent. History records that because Hindu women were a prime target of Islamic immigration, Hindu women of yore were terrified of them. They also found the invaders ugly and called them apes. But times have changed somewhat since then.

The Hindu is generally dark, with different shades of dark. The Brahmin who sits at the top of the caste totem pole is normally much fairer than the outcaste (untouchable), who exists beyond the pale. Such has been the case for millennia altogether. The Muslim invaders, especially the Afghans like Ghor were much fairer in skin than the average Hindu. They were not exactly white, but they were quite pale. When they started ruling over India, a noble at court had to be Muslim and fair-skinned.

There is a saying in India that the dark want to be fair and the fair fairer.

Twenty years ago, advertisements for fairness creams abounded on Indian television. Fair & Lovely, Fair & Beautiful, etc. Then a campaign, Dark is Beautiful, akin to the Black is Beautiful campaign in the US, was launched. It became politically incorrect to sell fairness creams. Today they still abound but under different guises. Creams to remove dark spots. But if the whole face is dark, the cream has perforce to be applied to the entire face.

Anti-tanning creams. The implication is obvious. The cream will prevent you from getting dark if you go out in the sun. It's funny. Tanning lotions have permeated the entire West but in India it's just the reverse. The Afghan invaders came to India with a very small train of people. India's population during the Ghori invasion was close to 100 million. It was all mainly Hindu. It must be noted that during the ensuing nearly six hundred years of Muslim rule, the Hindu population of India actually contracted. This is what foreign immigration does to you.

The Muslim rulers were scared that the Hindus would rebel and oust them. They built massive forts to protect themselves. But that was not enough. They needed a buffer between themselves and the Hindus. They had come to India to spread Islam. But the caste Hindus (who belong to the four upper castes in Hinduism) were very attached to their faith. The outcastes were oppressed under the caste system. They were attached to Hinduism but not so much. The Muslim rulers saw an opportunity here.

They targeted the outcastes with baskets of inducements were they to convert to Islam. Many resisted because Hinduism still ran strongly in their veins, so the sword was employed. Most of the Muslims of the subcontinent are converts from the Hindu outcastes. Once they gained the protection of the King's own religion (Islam), they started tormenting their former oppressors, the caste Hindus. This is the main reason for the hatred that exists between the Hindus and the Muslims of India even today. It runs so deep that it has not been able to be erased one wee little bit for 800 years. Hindu India and Muslim Pakistan are poised to obliterate each other with hundreds of nukes, therefore the enmity persists.

Muslim immigration in India had completely overturned India society topsy-turvy. But the dark-skinned Muslim convert from Hinduism had a problem. All perks and privileges derived from the Court, but to be a member of the Court or its beneficiary, he had to be pale. A mad scramble then started to fetch brides from Kashmir in the uppermost region of India, where everyone was fair. The Muslim convert decided that even if he could not be fair, his progeny with Kashmiri women would become so and therefore would have a chance of being welcomed at Court.

That's why one sees so many fair Muslims in India and Pakistan. Even though marriage between Hindu and Muslim is almost taboo, it happens, mostly between Muslim men and Hindu women. As explained earlier, a Muslim woman cannot marry outside the faith. It is considered *shirk* (forbidden) in Islam. So if you want to marry a Muslim woman, you have to convert to Islam beforehand. This is not acceptable to most Hindu men. That's why there are so few Hindu men-Muslim women marriages in India.

The converse is not true. Traditionally Muslim invaders captured Hindu women, raped them, in some cases converted them and even married them. This led to a real fear of the Muslim man among Hindu women. In one famous incidence, in the Indian state of Rajasthan, when the Hindu fort fell to a Muslim invader, 30,000 Hindu women ascended the funeral pyre in a mass suicide act which is called *Jauhar* so that they would not fall prey live to the invader.

Most Hindu women are then wary of Muslim men and their overtures. But there are some who find them handsome because they are fair and well-built due to constant meat-eating. I was talking to a Hindu woman once and asked her how she found Muslim men. I thought she would say something deprecatory. Instead she said that she found them very handsome.

The love-jihad phenomenon in India has invited a riposte from the Hindu right wing. They want to *Beti Bachao, Bahu Lao* (Stop their women from falling prey to Muslim men, get Muslim brides for their sons). But Bollywood sets India's trends, not any right wing party. Just recently, the actress Sonakshi Sinha, daughter of a top-flight Hindu actor of his time, Shatrughan Sinha, has married Zafar Iqbal, a small-time Muslim actor, against parental opposition.

Sonakshi grew up in a very Hindu environment. Her brothers are named Luv and Kush, two twins playing prominent characters in the Hindu epic, *Ramayana*, after which her father's house is named. But Sonakshi had her way. The marriage sent tremors through India. Sonakshi and Zafar were trolled so badly by Hindu trolls that they had to shut down the comments section of their Instagram account.

It's an interesting phenomenon. High-caste Hindus even today would not countenance marrying Hindu outcastes. But if the Hindu outcaste has converted to Islam, he becomes more respectable. During the time of the prophet, the Islamic vision included Christians and Jews. So Islam allows Muslim men to marry Jewish and Christian women and let the women retain their faith. Jews and Christians constitute what are called *dhimmi* races in Islam. The children though born out of the wedlock of a Muslim man and a dhimmi woman must be brought up as Muslim. This must be something to do with the Islamic intent of making the whole world Muslim.

Women not belonging to the dhimmi races are considered purely as slave women. If a Muslim man marries a slave woman, she must convert to Islam.

Where do Hindu women lie on the dhimmi-slave spectrum? They are certainly not dhimmi. That is the exclusive preserve of the Abrahamic women, Jews and Christians. Hindu women must then be slaves. The earlier Muslim invaders of India, the Afghans, brooked no opposition to conversion from Hindu women. The foremost emperor of the later Mughal dynasty, Akbar, wanted to marry high-caste Hindu women. He accorded them *dhimmi* status.

But how equipped was a temporal figure like an emperor to change the status of women who were ordained slaves by Islamic scripture? The line between spiritual and temporal has always been blurred in Islam. Remember that Prophet Muhammad too was a political leader. So Akbar got away with his act. Today, Hindu women in India like Sonakshi retain their religion upon marrying a Muslim. It will be interesting to see in which religion their kids are brought up.

A celebrated family in India is the Pataudi family. Mansur Ali Khan Pataudi, a Muslim, married one of the foremost Bollywood actresses of her time (the sixties), Sharmila Tagore, a Hindu. India was still reeling from the aftereffects of the Partition of the subcontinent in 1947. In India, Muslims were considered traitorous for having supported the creation of Pakistan and were treated as a fifth column for that country. As a matter of fact, they still are for many Hindus. But the sixties were a very conservative time from today.

Sharmila's marriage to Mansur stunned the country, especially as she converted to Islam, taking the Muslim name of Sakina. Sharmila was not just an actress, a profession disdained by many respectable Indians. She was also closely related to India's national poet, Rabindranath Tagore. Rabindranath is one of the greatest Indians ever born, just a peg below Gandhi. People speculated how long the Sharmila-Mansur marriage would last. But the marriage went the full distance until Mansur died in 2011.

Sharmila-Mansur begat three children, one boy, Saif, and two girls, Soha and Saba. Saif and Soha were very westernized; Saba a very conservative Muslim. Saif married Amrita, a Sikh woman almost twice his age. He converted her to Islam, but then divorced her after having two children with her, both brought up in the Islamic faith.

Saif found an Italian girlfriend, but after gallivanting around, set his eyes on Kareena Kapoor, an actress from the first family of Bollywood, the Hindu Kapoors. They got married in a civil ceremony. The vows were said holding a book together. It was either the Koran or the Bible (Kareena's mother, Babita, is Christian) but it was certainly not the Hindu Gita. Kareena did not covert. She follows Hindu rituals in which Saif participates. His conduct is heresy to many Muslims in India.

Kareena and Saif have two boys, Taimur and Jeh. Taimur was a thirteenth century Muslim marauder who had instilled fear in Europeans through the brutality of his murderous campaigns. He was lame in one leg, so he came to be known as Taimur the Lame in Europe. When he sacked Delhi, he killed everyone in the Hindu quarter. His memory still sends shivers down Indian spines.

How appropriate was it for Saif to name his son Taimur, knowing history? Saif feigned innocence, claiming that while he knew about the existence of Taimur, the real reason that he named his son as such was because Taimur means strong in Arabic. Saif knows that Taimur will be teased when he grows up, but he refuses to change his name.

Saif's sister, Soha, a Muslim, has married Kunal Khemu, a Hindu. It is unclear if Soha has converted to Hinduism, although she participates in Hindu rituals with her husband. They have one daughter---Inaaya Naumi Khemu Khan. Her first name is Persian-sounding and her last name, Khan, is very Muslim. It could be that Kunal has converted to Islam. Even if he hasn't, his daughter, Inaaya Khan, will be presumed to be Muslim because of her first and last names. Perhaps Kunal and Soha are raising Inaaya as Muslim.

But that's just the thing. When a Muslim man marries a Hindu woman, he asserts his religiosity over her and their children. When a Muslim woman marries a Hindu man, she asserts her religiosity over him and their children. Saif said that in no circumstances could he have given his boys Hindu names like Ram and Krishna. Why the hell not? You have been living in India for generations altogether, for centuries. Local names are still abhorrent to you. Why has your brother-in-law, Kunal, given his daughter an Islamic first name, Inaaya, and an Islamic last name, Khan. Even if she's raised Hindu, she will always be considered Muslim with the name Inaaya Khan.

The Shahi Imam (Royal Imam) of Delhi's main mosque, the Jama Masjid, was anointing his son in a grand ceremony as the *naib* (deputy) Imam of the mosque and his heir apparent in 2014. He invited the then prime minister of Pakistan, Nawaz Sharif, to the event but not the Indian prime minister, Narendra Modi. Granted that many Muslims have personal grouses against Modi, but to ignore the ruler of their own native land is near-blasphemous. The Shahi Imam calls himself Bukhari. He traces his lineage to Bukhara, a city in Uzbekistan.

His DNA might be all Indian now, but he still considers himself Uzbek. This is the classic immigrant's dilemma. Even after centuries of coming to India, many Muslims hark back to Persia and Arabia and Afghanistan and Turkey and Central Asia as their places of origination. If you do a DNA test, you will find that they have not even one percent foreign blood, that they are wholly Indian, but they refuse to believe it. For them, their ancestry will always remain foreign, not Hindu.

Even the Hindu convert to Islam acts as if his origins are non-Hindu. They give themselves foreign-sounding names and go about pretending that their lineage is all the way back to the prophet of Islam. After 3-4 generations of conversion, the Hindu convert has completely wiped out all traces of Hinduism in himself. He has even created a new language, Urdu, which is a mix of Hindi, Persian, and Arabic, and which is written in the Islamic script.

When the British left India, many Muslims were mad that they were not returning the country back to the people from whom they had seized it, the Muslims. Such Muslims were delusional. The British won India from the Hindu Marathas, who ruled over India from Delhi, in the eighteenth century. The Marathas had captured Delhi from the Muslim Mughals. Many Indian Muslims opposed the partition of India. They said that the people behind the partition movement were fools. Why were they only settling for one-third of the land when India in its entirety belonged to Muslims? For them, it was not a case of them belonging to India; it was a case of India belonging to them.

Many Indian Muslims still fantasize about what in their minds was the time of the glorious rule of Islam in India. It might have been glorious for them; it certainly was not for the majority Hindu population.

The experience of Muslims in India illustrates what I had written about earlier as the immigrant's dilemma. Where do I belong? Where are my roots? To which land do I owe my loyalty? How do I treat the indigenous people who have let me in? When do I become indigenous? When do I start considering myself indigenous? Do I consider my religion and way of life as superior to those of the indigenous people? How much of the country that I am immigrating to do I want to change? These questions have plagued societies with immigrants, have remained eternal and many still remain unanswered.

The Dutch East Company was the first European trader to come to India, followed by the British East India Company and the French. The British defeated the French in battle and sidelined both the French and the Dutch to small outposts in southern India. The Europeans ostensibly came as traders but were in fact marauders. They had armies of their own. The hold of the Mughal Empire in Delhi was weakening, so they saw their chance to wrest control of all of India.

The British focused on the east of India and established base in Calcutta (now Kolkata). Two key battles made the British entrenched in Bengal (of which Calcutta was the capital). The first one was in 1757 and is called the Battle of Plassey. It was a decisive victory of the British East India Company, under the leadership of Robert Clive, over the Nawab of Bengal and his French allies. Clive is known as the founder of the British Empire in India.

He carted away so much loot from India to England that he had to face a privy council inquiry in England. He told the judges, what I have brought with me is nothing if you had only seen what I could have brought. Clive was absolved. The second battle was the Battle of Buxar fought in 1764 in the Indian state of Bihar. The battle was once again decisively won by the British, extending their rule over the entire Ganges Valley, which now lay at the British East Company's mercy.

Once again we see how immigrants don a peaceful guise (traders) and stay to rule. Two hundred years of British rule transformed India. The British imposed English as the lingua franca of the country. Today, more than 100 million Indian speak fluent English, by many accounts better than the English themselves. A further 300 million speak pidgin English. One can get by in India without knowing any of the local languages and just by knowing English. If you are a foreigner and even if you speak accented English in India, you can happily get by. India had a prime minister, Rajiv Gandhi, who barely spoke Hindi but was fluent in English. Once he became PM, he had to take classes in Hindi so that he could address political rallies. Still, his Hindi remained shaky at best and was a source of constant mirth within the country.

The Hindu male has abandoned his traditional attire for the pant-shirt imposed by the British. Even his way of eating has changed. It is incumbent upon the Indian upper-class as well as the upper middle-class to learn how to use a knife and fork to eat. Lord Macaulay was a British politician who served in India in the first half of the nineteenth century. He made changes to the educational system in India. He claimed that a single shelf of a good European library was worth the whole native literature of India and Arabia. He imposed English on the Indians only to make them into clerks to run the British Empire. But the Indians were so smart that in a decade's time, they were reciting Chaucer back to the British.

In the 1700s, the British called Indians natives, in the 1800s *coolies* (porters), and in the 1900s, just plain niggers. The Prince of Wales (later Edward VIII and then Duke of Windsor) visited India in 1921along with his friend, Lord Mountbatten, later to become the Viceroy of India. Both the men were so liberal in using the word nigger for Indians that members of their entourage had to refrain them from doing so. Still, they went on and on.

Today much is made in the West about India's English language proficiency and how it has helped India in particularly the Information Technology sector. This is no doubt true. India hosted the G20 summit with great pomp and show in 2023 in Delhi. The G20 comprises the countries that have the world's top 20 economies. Much was made of the fact that India was now the fifth largest economy in the world. But the real marker to denote prosperity of a country is per capita income. India has the least per capita income in the G20, which includes many other Third World countries. When the British came to India, the country had 24% of the world's economy. When they left, India had only 2%. First Muslim rule, and then British rule, destroyed India over a period of roughly 800 years.

Gandhi said that no nation can prosper if they don't work and think in their own language. Look around. The US and the UK think and work in their native tongue, English; France in French; Germany in German; Japan in Japanese; China in Chinese. These comprise some of the wealthiest nations in the world. Can you think of a counter-example where a country that speaks in an alien language is prosperous? None will come to mind. India's elite, the 100-million English speaking class that controls the country, has propelled the country so far ahead prosperity-wise but no further.

The two clear markers of success in India are fair skin and proficiency in English. The fair skin aspiration was initially derived from the Muslim invaders and immigrants from places like Persia and then solidified under the British. English became important because of the British. If you are fair and speak good English, you have the best chance of success in India. If you are dark but speak good English, you still have hope. The same thing if you are fair and do not speak good English. But you are doomed if you are dark and not proficient in English. You might as well own a petty shop or some such business.

Just to encapsulate, immigrants whether they have been Muslim invaders and rulers or even otherwise peaceful immigrants from Persia, or the hoity-toity British, have completely transformed India, nay they have destroyed India—its religion, its culture, its mores, its languages, its prejudices, even its food. Immigration has done much harm to India. A country that was once called a golden bird is today amongst the poorest nations in the world. And it doesn't develop as fast as it should because it uses an imposed, foreign language, and its people still think how the immigrants of yore, especially the British, would have solved its present-day problems and therefore want to ape them.

Rapid progress is certainly not possible because those immigrants only devised solutions for their own benefit. Indians today need to creatively come up with their own answers.

3. **What immigration from Mexico and the Muslim world is doing to the US**

Immigration from Mexico is one of the most pervasive of all immigration to the US. To focus the discussion, attention is only being paid to immigration from Mexico, recognizing though that immigration from Central America is growing rapidly and has become a huge problem as well.

Mexicans are the largest group within the Latino population in the US, comprising two-thirds of the US Latino population of 55 million, which means there are about 37 million Mexicans in the US. Mexicans also constitute about 60% of the approximately 12 million undocumented people (illegal aliens or illegal immigrants) in the US. Most find jobs in the secondary labor market, where wages are anyway depressed. (The secondary labor market is the labor market consisting of high-turnover, low-pay jobs, and usually part-time or temporary work. Sometimes, secondary jobs are performed by high school or college students. The majority of service sector, light manufacturing, retail, and agricultural jobs are considered secondary labor.)

Further, because undocumented workers don't have their immigration papers in order, unscrupulous employers pay them even lower wages or sometimes nothing at all, knowing that the undocumented workers do not have access to law enforcement. What this double-whammy does is that it lowers wages in markets where illegal immigrants compete. Now one could say that these are markets where the native-born do not want to work in or will not work in, so the double whammy shouldn't affect them per se.

But then there are low-skilled, legal immigrants, many of them from Mexico itself. (In 2021, there were about 10.7 million Mexican-born individuals living in the United States. About 7 million were illegal, so about **4 million were legalized Mexican immigrants.**)

These low-skilled, legal immigrants compete in the same markets as the illegals, and have to bear with the low wages caused by the presence of the illegals.

But it is not only the secondary labor market where wage depression occurs. It happens in primary labor markets like IT. I used to work as a product marketing manager for Dell in Austin, Texas. I was there working on the training part of my student visa. The student visa was supposed to transition to an H-1B work visa. I had a master's degree in electrical engineering, so had to be paid a certain amount based on the prevailing wage rate.

But my one-year training period was ending and my H-1B still hadn't come. The visa officer at Dell explained that my application for the H-1B had been rejected because they were paying me about $5,000 less than the prevailing wage rate. And this was Austin in 1999, were wages were already low then. The officer explained that were I to lose my visa status, I would have to leave the job, and then be rehired when the corrected H-1B arrived. That could take months.

Sitting on the sidelines would not have been fun. In addition, I was not in the good books of my boss, in part because I was dating a white woman at work. She was a hot commodity and I know that many white males in the office felt how had a darkie like me been able to snag her. Once I went out of status, my boss could have let go of me easily. I would then have to leave for India, leaving behind my girlfriend, to whom I was considering getting married.

Mercifully, the H-1B came in the nick of time. But it was only small mercies really. My boss fired me the next month. I had to find another job in 10 days or leave the country.

Luckily I found a job in California. My girlfriend did not want to move to California, so that meant the end of our relationship. This example exemplifies how even high-skilled legal workers are being exploited by unscrupulous employers and the impact that unscrupulousness can have on people's lives. Twenty-one years later, and I still pine for my Austin girlfriend. I am still single, hoping and praying that she'll come back to me.

It is not only H1-Bs where scams are taking place and where native-born Americans have to face competition from foreigners doing work on depressed wages. It is also in the coveted green card, also known as permanent residency, process. Dell in 2000 had an employee strength of 40,000. One-quarter of these must have been foreigners. To handle visa affairs of 10,000 people, Dell had only two officers. There was no hope in hell that Dell was going to get me my green card.

My immigration lawyer cautioned me. He said that without the green card, you are just an economic slave in the US. He added that I should not seek employment in big companies like Cisco, Intel or Oracle. He said that they have a very large proportion of foreign workers, mostly Indian and Chinese, and do everything to delay their green cards. Green cards there could take even more than 5 years to come. In the meantime, the employee would not be promoted or given any wage increase because the company knew that it had its shackles on him.

My lawyer counseled that I seek a small company and get an assurance in writing from them that they would get me my green card, and that too in the fast-track way. A small company's VP of HR immediately consented but then tried to backtrack. I would have none of it so he gave me the signed assurance. When companies delay obtaining the green card for an employee, they are keeping their wage bill low. The employee is a slave because he cannot move to another company without starting the green card process afresh. This way they are making sure that the foreign employee sticks to them, is worked to death and is denied promotions. They could have hired a native-born American and provided him real wages and growth prospects, but they refuse to do so.

Native-born Americans suffer as there is a ready and willing foreign slave force ready to comply with the bullying and the harassment of these companies. These are not everyday journeyman companies. They are the crème de la crème of the American corporate sector. Their CEOs go round the world lecturing on corporate ethics but direct malafide practices at home. Even the US government looks the other way. What matters is the profitability of the economy. Paeans are sung about the benefit that H-1B foreign workers are bringing to the US economy but not a tear is shed for the native-born American worker. He is seen as too expensive, too unskilled, too assertive.

A constant gripe in the US is that Americans are shying away from STEM (science, technology, engineering, math) studies that lead to high-paying jobs. But if the American student knows that the space at the end of the grueling STEM tunnel is already clogged up with cheap foreign workers and that no light comes in through for him, then why would he attempt the STEM route? It's a simple dynamic of supply and demand. American policy-makers must stop or stall the H-1B program, so that native Americans can get a chance. It is made out as if the Indian and Chinese students are brilliant and that American students don't hold a candle to them. But if you see some of the major tech companies—Google, Apple, Amazon, Facebook, or Microsoft—they were all founded and built by Americans. I cannot think a major American company that was founded and built by foreigners. Foreigners can ride well on what Americans have built but they cannot innovate from the ground-up and build significant companies. So this thesis that foreigners are smarter than Americans is entirely wrong. If the foreigners—the Indians and the Chinese—were so smart, they why don't they stay back in their home countries and build them? Why do they have come to America's shores and seemingly work wonders and go gaga about it? In conversation with many foreign workers, they will tell you how much smarter they are than native Americans, who they actually call dumb. They do not consider themselves cheaper, but in effect, they are. They consider themselves faster and better, which they or may not be. IT companies pride on producing products cheaper, faster, better, but their own employees may not be the same.

Crime is what drives many Mexican emigres out of Mexico. Crime, poverty, drug cartels, extortion, kidnapping, ransom, murder, the whole nine yards. The whole country is awash in crime. Poor Mexicans have nowhere to look at other than their northern border with the US. Drug use is high in the US, higher than in Mexico. Many Americans seem to have become addicted to cannabis and cocaine and heroin and lately, fentanyl and methamphetamine. The US State department estimated that 90% of cocaine entering the US is produced in Colombia, followed by Bolivia and Peru, and that the main transit route is through Mexico.

Drug cartels in Mexico control approximately 70% of the foreign narcotics flow into the United States. Drug cartels distribute Asian methamphetamine to the US. It is believed that almost half of the cartels' revenues come from cannabis. Cocaine and heroin are also traded, and increasingly so fentanyl. Although Mexico accounts for only a small share of worldwide heroin production, it supplies a large share of the heroin distributed in the US.

It would not be false to say that Mexico is the drug gateway of choice for the US, and that immigrants employed by the cartels carry on the trade. Stanching the Mexican people inflow into the US will also drastically decrease the drug trade.

But it's all a question of supply and demand. Drugs are killing the US, but there is a strong demand for them. US politicians will not get elected if they stop the drug supply. Very often US politicians themselves are culpable in taking drugs. Bill Clinton said that he smoked, but didn't inhale. Barack Obama openly joked about having marijuana. He was talking about a company called Buzzfeed, and laughed that that's what he had at night in college. Michele Obama was sitting nearby, and she too laughed. There is intense debate in the US whether cannabis is a drug or not. Many states, including California, have made it legal to smoke and produce.

Wherever there is money to be made from the drug trade, Mexican cartels do not lag behind. Since 2003, Mexican cartels have used the dense, isolated portions of US federal and state parks and forests to grow marijuana under the canopy of thick trees. Billions of dollars' worth of marijuana is being produced annually on U.S. soil. In 2006, federal and state authorities seized over 550,000 marijuana plants worth an estimated one billion dollars in Kentucky's remote Appalachian counties. Cartels profited from marijuana growing operations from Arkansas to Hawaii.

Mexican immigrants (legal and illegal) sent home more than $54.1 billion in remittances via formal channels in 2021, according to the World Bank, the vast majority undoubtedly from the United States. Global remittances represented about 4% of Mexico's gross domestic product (GDP) in 2021. (The United States is overwhelmingly the most popular destination for Mexicans living abroad, accounting for 97% of all Mexican emigrants. In fact, 8% of all people born in Mexico lived in the United States as of 2020. Canada is home to the next largest population of Mexicans (87,000), followed by Spain (61,000), Germany (20,000), and Guatemala (19,000), according to mid-2020 United Nations Population Division estimates.)

While this money helps meet the basic needs of millions of Mexican families back home, it is also money that is lost from the US economy. Mexican officials in the 1960s discouraged emigration in the 1960s, but by the 1970s, those same officials encouraged the departure of working-class men as a solution to high unemployment and population growth in the country, and to earn remittances from the US.

In 1 986, the US Congress passed the Immigration Reform and Control Act, making it more difficult to cross borders. By then, however, undocumented migration had already become a self-perpetuating phenomenon. In light of the new hardships of migration, many Mexican families decided to settle together in the United States and dared not return to Mexico for fear that they would not be able to get back into the United States. They now felt entrapped in the United States, which they referred to as the *jaula de oro*, or the "golden cage."

Since the 1970s, Mexican migrants have been accused of abusing welfare, increasing crime, taking jobs away from US citizens and bearing children in the United States. These may be myths but they are stereotypes that are firmly implanted in the native mind.

The illegal entry to the US, via its southern border, of an estimated 500,000 people each year (from October 2022 to October 2023, some 2.2 million migrants had crossed into the

US from its southern border) has led the US government to start building a security fence along the most sensitive areas. Occasionally, tensions have risen between Mexican immigrants on the one hand and Americans and other ethnic groups on the other because of increasing concerns over the availability of working-class jobs to Americans and immigrants from other ethnic groups. Opposition to illegal immigration has been reflected in the emergence of Minutemen groups—American citizens who have taken it upon themselves to patrol the US borders and to confront illegal workers in cities around the US. Just imagine, militiamen going around the US-Mexican border ready to shoot whom they deem to be illegal migrants, as well as shooting and beating Mexicans whom they accost in American cities whom they believe not to have their papers. Is this the image of itself that the US wants to send out to the world at large?

 While Donald Trump's wall, loaded with sensors et al, came in for much criticism, it probably is one of the best ways to curb illegal migration. Congresswoman Alexandra Ocasio-Cortez, who is of Latino heritage, and who is a firebrand on the extreme left of the Democratic Party with undue influence over the Biden administration in most matters, visited Trump's wall and threw a hissy fit there, screaming tear down this wall. Instead of tearing down the wall, Biden has been compelled to build more of his own to stem the tide of refugees from the southern border. Now with the advent of Artificial Intelligence, it might possible to build a really sophisticated wall all along the southern border.

And there is a human rights issue as well. Hundreds of illegal immigrants who cross into the US from Mexico have died in the scorching heat of the Arizona desert. And these young Mexican adults, the cream of Mexican society, who are migrating, not the old and the infirm. When they leave Mexico, ageing communities are left behind. With fewer children, these communities will gradually die out. There are bodies of dead Latino children floating in the Rio Grande. What if these young migrants were made to stay back in Mexico and build their own country? You would not see the horrific deaths that we are witnessing today.

A common opinion among Americans is the belief that the United States is a "welfare magnet," which attracts immigrants seeking to acquire access to generous public benefits. The economist Milton Friedman, who argued for a libertarian position, holds that open immigration would be optimal economically if it were not for the welfare state. As he put it, "It's just obvious that you cannot have free immigration and a welfare state." Interestingly, there is a liberal version of the same argument. Former Colorado Governor Richard D. Lamm, a Democrat, argued that: Social and redistributive programs require borders. It is fine to think of yourself as a citizen of the world, but we solve most problems in a national context and therefore we owe a greater moral duty to our fellow Americans than we do to non-citizens. Liberals must defend borders or they will lose all the social programs that they care about! No social program can survive without geographic limits and defined beneficiaries.

American workers with lower educations are more likely than those with higher educations to support restrictionist immigration policies. Even those with higher educations, in states where the fiscal burden from immigration is large tend to favor restrictionist policies because their taxes are higher as a result of immigration. (There is no doubt that immigrants, both legal and illegal, use public services, which cost taxpayer dollars. The costs of immigration are called the fiscal burden.)

Some additional facts about Mexican immigrants follow. Mexican immigrants are less likely to be proficient in English than the overall foreign-born population. In 2021, about 65% of Mexicans ages five and over reported limited English proficiency, compared to about 46% of all immigrants. Approximately 6% of Mexican immigrants spoke only English at home, versus 17% of all immigrants. Mexican adults have much lower rates of educational attainment than both the native- and overall foreign-born populations. In 2021, approximately 52% of Mexican immigrants ages 25 and older lacked a high school diploma or equivalent, compared to 26% of foreign-born adults and 7% of US-born adults. About 9% of Mexican immigrants reported having a bachelor's degree or higher, compared to 35% of US-born and 34% of immigrant adults.

On average, Mexicans have lower incomes than the overall foreign- and native-born populations. In 2021, households headed by a Mexican immigrant had a median annual income of $56,000, compared to $70,000 for all immigrant- and native-led households. In 2021, Mexican immigrants were more likely to be in poverty (17%) than immigrants overall (14%) or the US born (13%).

Mexicans are much less likely to be naturalized US citizens than immigrants overall. In 2021, 35% of Mexican immigrants were US citizens, compared to 53% of the total foreign-born population. This could be because of a combination of factors: Mexicans prize their Mexican citizenship more than the US one and/or the path to naturalization for Mexicans could be tougher because so many of them are illegal immigrants and/or because of their poor education and the high cost of the naturalization process and/or Mexican immigrants are just tardy in obtaining US citizenship.

Mexican immigrants are the largest group participating in the Deferred Action for Childhood Arrivals (DACA) program, which provides temporary deportation relief and work authorization to unauthorized migrants who arrived as children and meet the program's education and other eligibility criteria. As of mid-2022, 480,200 Mexicans were active DACA participants, accounting for the vast majority of all 594,100 DACA recipients, according to U.S. Citizenship and Immigration Services (USCIS) data.

I might be boring you with too many facts and figures, but it is only to reinforce the commonly-held perceptions about Mexican immigrants. Yes, they are dirt-poor to start with, their journey from Mexico to the US is perilous at best, their life in the US perhaps even harder, but almost on every metric they score lower than immigrants from other countries and the US-born, whether it be education, English language fluency, income levels, rates of naturalization (US-born do not count here), or access to welfare schemes like DACA.

Is this the kind of population that we want to let into the US? There is the fear of a real dumbing down of the American population here. Overwhelmingly (97%) of world's Mexican immigrants reside in the US. What does that do to our competitive situation with other G7 countries and China? Yes, Mexican immigrants bring substantive things to the party, but do not the costs of having them here in the US outweigh the benefits?

Muslim Americans are estimated at 3.45 million people of all ages, with 2.15 million being adults. Fifty-eight percent of Muslim Americans are first-generation immigrants, being born in another country. Forty-two percent are those that are born in the US. Since

this work is about immigration, let us just focus on the 58% of Muslims that are born outside the US.

Pakistan sends by the largest share of Muslim immigrants to the US at 9% of the overall Muslim population, while Iran is at 6%, and India and Afghanistan at 4% each. Overall, South Asia sends the most Muslim immigrants (at 20%) followed by Middle East/North Africa (at 14%). Muslims bring a rich diversity to America's shores, but look carefully at the composition of where the Muslims are emanating from, and you will see a disturbing pattern.

While the powers that be in Pakistan are not openly hostile to the US, the Pakistani population often is. As of 2014, 59% of Pakistanis consider the United States to be an enemy, a number reduced from 74% in 2012. The Pakistanis have the least favorable view of US compared with 39 countries in the world surveyed by Pew. The factors behind this orientation of Pakistanis to the US is myriad.

Above all, it is religious. Pakistan is an overwhelmingly Muslim country that sees the Christian US as infidel. Tolerance for extremism and anti-American terror groups in Pakistan is high. The Pakistanis felt jilted by the US after the Afghan jihad against the Soviet Union, because the Americans quickly decamped from the region. The Pakistanis felt betrayed because they had to bear the brunt of the Afghani mess. Note that the role of the Saudi Arabians was akin to that of the Americans during the war; they both supplied money and arms to the Afghan and Pakistani fighters.

The Saudis too exited the arena quickly once the Soviets quit, but the Pakistanis don't hold the Saudis in poor esteem. They didn't feel abandoned by the Saudis as they did by the Americans. This is because the Saudis are Muslim, in fact they are the fountainhead

of Islam, so the Pakistanis dare not go against them. In fact, once Bin Laden ensconced

himself in Afghanistan, the Pakistanis were supposed to have known of his location but

refused to share it with the West. Bill Clinton launched Tomahawk cruise missiles in

August 1998 against the Khost province in Afghanistan, where Bin Laden was supposed

to be located.

The missiles were to fly over Pakistan en route to Afghanistan. The Americans made the

mistake of informing the Pakistanis that they were the ones sending these missiles, just in

case the Pakistanis thought that the Indians were doing so, which would have sparked an

all-out war between the two countries. In the 10-15 minutes that it took the missiles to

reach their target, Bin Laden had already vamoosed from the target area because the

Pakistanis had intimated him about the oncoming missiles. Imagine if Bin Laden would

have been decapitated in 1998. There would have been no 9/11, no war in Afghanistan or

Iraq, no nothing.

Most Muslim immigrants in the US are peaceful and comply with US law. But a few are

not able to overcome the historical animosity between Islam and Christianity, as well as

between Islam and Judaism. Consider the recent attacks on Israel that Hamas launched in

2023, and which took the lives of over 1,200 innocent Israeli civilians, with about 300-

400 being taken hostage. This was an outrage of the highest magnitude. Israel was bound

to respond, and it did so disproportionately. US campuses, including the trend-setting Ivy

Leagues, erupted with Muslim students as well as their American compatriots protesting

the Israeli action. Lost in the din was what the Muslim Hamas had done to the Jewish

Israel.

Some powers that be in the US pride themselves on diversity. If you speak to the layman, you might get a different reaction. Islam has been at odds with Christianity and Judaism ever since its inception 1,400 years ago. The animosity is deep-seated and visceral. One of the founding principles of Islam is to spread the faith. A Muslim is enjoined to do so wherever he is, whether he lives in a Muslim-majority country like Pakistan or Saudi Arabia, or whether he lives in a Muslim-minority country like the US or India. That's where the rift comes in. Most Christians, Jews, Hindus, and Buddhists are happy with their faith. They don't see any merit in converting to another faith.

Islam claims itself to be the most superior religion in the world. But I don't see the logic of referring to holy books and what is inside them. I look at the practitioners of the religion. Consider Christianity. While Christianity has had a violent past, today it is the Christian West that most people from the Third World aspire to emigrate to. 1990 found me doing a PhD on a university scholarship at Purdue University in the US. My roommate, also doing a PhD on a university scholarship, exclaimed: It must be the love taught in Christianity that allows Americans to let in and support so many foreigners.

What example are the practitioners of Islam setting? Was 9/11 justified? Among four demands, Bin Laden's key demand was the amelioration of the way in which Israel and the US treated Palestinians. Granted, there could have been much improvement made in this regard. But was this demand sufficient to kill over 3,000 people, destroy a city, demolish a government structure (the Pentagon) and crash four planes. Bin Laden knew then that if he succeeded in his plans, he would invite the fury of the US, just as Hamas with its more recent strike on Israel knew that fierce retribution will follow. Bin Laden's and Hamas's intention was to escalate, and escalate the US and Israel did, and look where the Muslim world, places like Gaza and countries like Afghanistan, Iraq, Syria, Yemen, and Libya are now.

Strict law enforcement has prevented a strike on a major scale in the US. But both Pakistan and Iran (probably) have nuclear weapons. Revenge for the destruction of the aforementioned places is burning in many a jihadi heart. Pakistan has many tactical loose nukes floating around. What will it take for a bunch of jihadis to get their hands on a loose nuke and then burst it in the US? The US would go mad in response. The world would be facing Armageddon.

Why is that most immigrants in the US who are implicated in acts of terrorism are Muslim? The Pakistani, Faisal Shahzad, set up a car bomb to blow up Times Square in 2010. More recently, in 2022, Hadi Matar, stabbed the novelist Salman Rushdie. Matar was born in California to parents who emigrated from Yaroun in the south of Lebanon, a mixed Shia-Christian village where support for Hezbollah and the Iranian government is high. The Iranian government denied any involvement in the attack, although state-controlled media celebrated it.

In 1989, Iran's then supreme leader, Ayatollah Khomeini, had issued a fatwa against Rushdie for a book that Rushdie wrote, *The Satanic Verses*, which Khomeini deemed insulted the prophet of Islam. In 1998, the government of Iran looked to distance itself from the fatwa and pledged no longer to urge that it be carried out. In 2017, however, the current supreme leader of Iran, Ayatollah Ali Khamenei, reaffirmed that the edict remained in effect, saying, "The decree is as Imam Khomeini issued."

Rushdie lost the use of one eye and one hand in the stabbing. Rushdie wrote a memoir about the attack, *Knife: Meditations After an Attempted Murder*.

Muslim Pakistanis in Pakistan are taught to hate Hindus and the Hindu religion. They would never assume a Hindu identity while in Pakistan. But once they are in the US, and realizing what a bad rap Muslim names like Muhammed, Abdullah and Khan are getting, they hide behind Hindu names. The problem is that Pakistanis and Indians look the same. Every time there is a terror incident in the West involving a Pakistani, Hindus too get the rap. I myself have been called terrorist many times in the US, once by the senior vice president of a company I worked for in Silicon Valley.

I was clean shaven at the time. Mightily offended, I grew a moustache to reinforce my "terrorist" identity. Finally, the senior vice president said, enough, you can go back to your clean shaven ways. South Asian immigrants constitute 20% of the Muslim population of the US; Middle Easterners and North Africans another 14%. It takes only one or two individuals to get provoked to commit a terrorist act.

Islam forbids drink and dance and music, so the mosque is the fount of religious and cultural activities for Muslims. Fridays are special prayer days for Muslims. The Imam of a mosque leads the prayers and then gives his sermon. Because his sermon is purportedly based on the Koran, or the word of god, his flock takes his words very seriously. If an atrocity happens against Muslims anywhere in the world, the Imam can take note of that. Radical Imams go even further. They counsel revenge against any action against the Muslim *ummah* (world). The FBI has had its informers in many mosques to learn what the Imams are preaching, but it cannot be everywhere.

Of all immigrants to the US, Muslim immigrants find it the hardest to integrate. This is about the peculiar nature of Islam itself. Islam allows Muslim men to marry *dhimmi* women, specifically Christians and Jews. The women can keep their faith, but the offspring of any such union must be raised Muslim. This is unacceptable to many American women. Furthermore, a Muslim woman cannot marry outside the faith. So any non-Muslim man interested in a Muslim woman has to convert to Islam. This again is abhorrent to most men.

Islam prohibits drinking, although many Muslim men drink, some on the sly. American culture is centered around drinking and partying. All American festivities involve drinking. So once again Muslims find it hard to assimilate into American culture. Music and dance and movies too are integral to American life. These are forbidden in Islam. Other differences also emerge. Muslims don't eat pork, a favorite American food. Meat consumed by Muslims must be *halal* (slaughtered in a certain way), whereas Americans don't care. The first thing that an orthodox Muslim will ask in a restaurant is if the meat is *halal.*

But nowhere do Muslims and Americans differ as much as in the treatment of women. Women are subservient beings in Islam. This was not always the case. At the time of the prophet, and after his passing, women took prominent roles. At the forefront was his wife, Ayesha. But sharia law, over time, has overturned the status of Muslim women. American women cannot fathom how Muslim women dress in a full-faced black burqa in the searing heat of an Arizona or Texas. Less educated Muslim immigrants are more keen to follow the sharia. If a less educated Muslim immigrant would marry an American woman, he would tend to put her in a burqa, or some other conventional Muslim dress.

The US is secular; the separation of church and state is clear. Most Muslim immigrants come from societies where Muslims preponderate and where sharia law is enforced. They cannot fathom that a law other than that guided by Islam can be imposed. US consulates do little vetting or even information sessions warning would-be arrivals to the US just how different it is and to be prepared for culture shock. More importantly, they do not counsel the new immigrants not to try to change the customs of America. America is a fiercely Christian nation. Many Muslims in America start proselytizing i.e. spreading their faith.

This meets with intense resistance, even hatred, in America. Firstly, Christianity, like Islam, believes that it is the only path to god. Secondly, Christians can be as evangelical as Muslims. But Christian nations like the US have evolved over time to accommodate every religion. The people have become tolerant too. But in general they do not like to be converted to another faith, especially a faith as rigid and obscurantist as Islam. Muslim immigrants in the US would be wise to practice their faith quietly and not make waves to increase their flock by convincing Americans how pure Islam is.

This chapter has talked about Mexican immigration as well as Muslim immigration to the US. Poverty and the promise of a better life in America are the common factors why both groups immigrate to the US. But while most of the Mexican immigrants are Christian and integrate better in a predominantly Christian country like America, Muslim immigrants because of their different faith find it hard to do so. Immigrants do jobs that natives are loathe to do or cannot do.

For instance, I met a black woman in Atlanta who obviously was not very smart. She said she saw an Indian with a Bentley; how come he was driving it and not her? I thought to myself, that perhaps the Indian works hard and smart. I used to play basketball with a bunch of black men in Atlanta. They thought that I worked at a gas station because in Atlanta many Indians follow that profession. They also thought that I was tight-fisted. I wondered, if only they would stop playing basketball all half-day and snorting cocaine the rest of the day, perhaps they too could make something of themselves. Gas stations pay poorly, but at least you are earning something.

That's precisely my point. Low-skilled immigration has made Americans lazy. They are disdaining the jobs that even a generation ago were acceptable to their forebears. High-skilled immigration is also putting stress on the system. Many Americans are not able to cope with STEM (science technology engineering math) immigrants. They feel that the jobs will go to the immigrant anyway, whiz kids as many of them are. So they do not even endeavor to pursue STEM fields. Why do something that has no future in it for you.

Overall, then the American population is suffering from Mexican as well as Muslim immigration. The pain is not just economic; it is also a marked change in the cultural and religious landscape of the country. If Mexican and Muslim immigration were to be ended, the country will self-correct to ultimately benefit all Americans.

4. What immigration is doing to Europe

The Netherlands is a small country: 41,865 km^2, 16,164 sq mi. With 18 million people, it is bursting at the seams. Its population density is 520/km^2 (1,347/sq mi). Students, workers, and asylum-seekers qualify as immigrants to the Netherlands. In 2022, 403,108 persons immigrated to the Netherlands. This was 150,580 more than the figure for 2021. In addition, 179,310 persons emigrated from the Netherlands, 33,980 more than one year earlier. Overall in 2022, more people migrated to the Netherlands than emigrated. Net migration (immigration minus emigration) amounted to 223,798 persons.

This level of net migration has caused alarm bells to ring in the country. Geert Wilders is one of the most rightwing politicians in the country. He leads the Party for Freedom, which he founded in 2006. In the last Dutch parliamentary elections in 2023, his party secured a plurality of seats, 37 out of a maximum possible 150 seats.

Wilders is best known for his criticism of Islam, summing up his views by saying, "I don't hate Muslims, I hate Islam". Although identifying Islamic extremists as 5–15% of Muslims, he argues that "there is no such thing as 'moderate Islam.'" He suggests that Muslims should "tear out half of the Koran if they wished to stay in the Netherlands" because it contains "terrible things" and that Muhammad would "... in these days be hunted down as a terrorist."

On 8 August 2007, Wilders opined in an open letter to the Dutch newspaper *De Volkskrant* that the Koran, which he called a "fascist book," should be outlawed in the Netherlands, like Adolf Hitler's *Mein Kampf.* He believes that all Muslim immigration to the Netherlands should be halted and all settled immigrants should be paid to leave. Referring to the increased population of Muslims in the Netherlands, he has said:

You no longer feel like you are living in your own country. Before you know it there will be more mosques than churches!

In a speech before the Dutch Parliament, he stated: "Islam is the Trojan Horse in Europe. If we do not stop Islamification now, Eurabia and Netherabia will just be a matter of time. One century ago, there were approximately 50 Muslims in the Netherlands. Today, there are about 1 million Muslims in this country. Where will it end? We are heading for the end of European and Dutch civilization as we know it. Very many Dutch citizens experience the presence of Islam around them. They have had enough of burkas, headscarves, the ritual slaughter of animals, so-called honor revenge, blaring minarets, female circumcision, hymen restoration operations, abuse of homosexuals, Turkish and Arabic on the buses and trains as well as on town hall leaflets, halal meat at grocery shops and department stores, Sharia exams, Sharia mortgages, and the enormous overrepresentation of Muslims in the area of crime, including Moroccan street terrorists."

Wilders speaks well, even if he exaggerates. His views are striking a chord with the people. He dreamt of being prime minister, but he needed a coalition to govern. His coalition partners, all rightwing parties, refused to countenance his anti-Islamic views. So he came up with a manifesto for the new government, entitled "Hope, Courage and Pride," which introduces strict measures on asylum-seekers, scraps family reunification for refugees and seeks to reduce the number of international students studying in the country.

Wilders settled on Dick Schoof, a former Dutch spy chief and current head of the Justice ministry, as prime minister. Schoof says that he won't kowtow to Wilders, but leftwing opposition leader Frans Timmermans described him as "emphatically Wilders' candidate." Schoof has sworn to implement Wilders' manifesto. He has vowed the "strictest-ever admission policy for asylum and the most comprehensive package for getting a grip on immigration." "Immigration puts too much pressure on social services and social cohesion. The asylum and immigration figures are high and so is the pressure on society," Schoof told Dutch lawmakers.

So there you are. A small but influential country in Europe, the Netherlands, is now firmly in the grip of immigration haters (even despising international students) and Islamophobists. Are they going to eject all Muslims from their country, as they have promised? Are they going to stop immigration altogether? The Dutch people were always known as a friendly and open people. Wilders promises to make the Netherlands less inviting to people of color, especially from Africa and Asia, than any other European country. But this is what happens with unchecked immigration. A small country gets swamped and then reacts ferociously to maintain its identity.

Let's look over and see what's happening in Italy. Giorgia Meloni is the prime minister of Italy. She, a woman, strangely leads a far-right party called Brothers of Italy. She is an admirer of Mussolini, claiming that whatever he did was in the interests of Italy. Meloni supports a naval blockade to halt immigration (because Italy has been inundated by migrants from the sea), and she has been accused of xenophobia and Islamophobia. She is opposed to birthright citizenship proposals, which would give citizenship including education rights to foreigners born and living in Italy. She has linked illegal immigration to crime, and refugee arrivals to human trafficking and prostitution.

Meloni has supported giving refugee status to Ukrainians in the wake of the Russo-Ukrainian War mainly because they are white and Christian. In 2018, she said that she would welcome Venezuelans, saying there are Christians and are often of Italian origins. So migration in Italy has two rules: one for white, Christian people, and the other for nonwhites. Immigration is therefore blinkered in its view. Meloni has endorsed the Great Replacement, a white nationalist conspiracy theory. She also believes there is a planned mass migration from Africa to Europe for the purpose of replacing and eliminating Italians, an anti-Semitic, white genocidal, and far-right conspiracy theory known as the Kalergi Plan. In January 2017, she called immigration to Italy "ethnic substitution."

Meloni complained about the danger of ethnic substitution also in her 2019 book on the Nigerian mafia, co-written with Alessandro Meluzzi, an anti-vaccine psychiatrist and founder of the "Anti-Islamization Party" and at the time primate of a schismatic Italian Orthodox Church. Along with other white supremacist stereotypes, the book argues that a project is underway to "change the European ethnicity and create Eurafrica," that the Nigerian mafia is the product of "local cultures that practice ritual murder and cannibalism," and that "the corpses of white people are very appreciated" by the Yoruba (people who belong to Nigeria), who are said to be engaged in the trade of human flesh and organs.

This is a woman feted in world capitals today. Meloni tried to make a deal with Tunisian President Kais Saied, with a focus on stopping illegal migration from Tunisia to Europe. In September 2023, more than 120 boats carrying around 7,000 migrants from Africa arrived on the Italian island of Lampedusa within 24 hours, increasing the volume handled by the local migration reception center by 15 times and leading to the migrants outnumbering the island's native population. Even in times of sorrow, Meloni carries a stern warning.

On February 26, 2023, a boat carrying migrants sank amidst harsh weather conditions while trying to land on the coast of Steccato di Cutro, near Crotone in the region of Calabria in Italy. The boat was carrying between 143 and 200 migrants when it sank, of whom at least 86 died, including 12 children, becoming one of the deadliest naval disasters in recent years. Meloni expressed her "deep sorrow for the many human lives torn away by human traffickers," and condemned the "exchange" of migrants' lives for "the 'price' of a ticket paid by them in the false prospect for a safe voyage."

According to Eurostat, in 2023, Italy's total population was 59 million. The total foreign-born was 6.4 million, which constituted 11% of the overall population. People born in an EU state were 1.5 million, or 2.6% of the overall population, and people born in a non-EU state were 4.9 million, or 8.2% of the overall population. It is the latter that Meloni wants to target and discriminate against mainly because they are nonwhite and non-Christian. She feels that their values and customs do not align with Italian values and customs and some of them might even enjoy eating Italians because they are white.

As the king (in this case, the queen), so the people, goes an old Indian saying. Or, if you prefer to go the English way, a people get the king they deserve. Public opinion in Italy regarding immigration aligns fairly and squarely with what Meloni thinks. No wonder she is a popular leader in Italy. In 2018, a poll by Pew Research found that a majority of Italians (71%) wanted fewer immigrants to be allowed into the country, 18% wanted to keep the current level and 5% wanted to increase immigration.

A 2019 poll by *YouGov* showed that 53% thought authorities should not accept more refugees from conflict areas, 25% were in favor of more refugees and 19% were undecided. According to a poll published by *Corriere della Sera* in 2019, one of two respondents (51%) approved closing Italy's ports to further boat migrants arriving via the Mediterranean, while 19% welcomed further boat migrants. In 2021, 77% of Italians thought the current immigrant influx was too high, as underlined by a poll published by *La Repubblica* and carried out by *YouGov*.

Once in Italy, the EU **Dublin Regulation** requires migrants to apply for legal residence, protection or asylum permits in the first EU country they cross into, effectively barring them from legally crossing internal EU borders until their case has been processed and positively concluded. As the vast majority of migrant people landing in Italy targets destinations in Central and Northern European States, there is a tendency to avoid filing permits applications in Italy and rather try a northwards land journey. That is the irony of it all. Italy and Greece are just used as waystations by migrants who would much rather make it to richer, more welcoming countries like Germany, France, and the UK rather than stay in economic backwaters and hostile environments like Italy and Greece. And that is getting Meloni hot and bothered under her collar.

Meloni should just let the migrants through. Lost in this saga about how Europe is affected by "white man-eating cannibals," is the sorry state of the boat people, thousands of whom try to cross the Mediterranean Sea every month to Italy in unsafe rubber dinghies, fishing trawlers, boats and rafts, otherwise hardly seaworthy, and generally vastly filled above their capacity. Official reports list boats filled up to two or three times nominal capacity, including rubber dinghies. This has led to several accidents at sea, as in

2007 (53 perished in one accident), 2009 (close to 500 dead or missing at sea in two accidents), 2011 (at least 150 people dead in an accident), 2013 (approximately 400 dead in an accident), 2014 (over 3,500 people perished in the whole year) and 2015 (more than 4,000 dead or missing in the whole year). 2016 was the worst year, with over 5,000 deaths and disappearances at sea. 30,001 missing migrants (deaths and disappearances at sea) have been recorded by the Missing Migrants Project since 2014 in the Mediterranean Sea. As collecting information is challenging, all figures remain undercounted.

These accidents became harder to document between 2014 and 2017, as people-smuggling organizations changed their tactics: instead of aiming for a full crossing of the sea towards Italy, their boats aimed just to exit Libyan territorial waters and then trigger rescue operation from passing mercantile vessels, seek and rescue organizations, and Italian and Maltese coastguards and militaries. As per the United Nations Convention of the Sea, of which Italy is a subscriber, people rescued at sea have to be transported to the closest safe harbor: as Libya continues to be in political turmoil this means they are transported to Italy. But what if no one at sea volunteers to rescue these boat people? They then would in the same predicament as before, which is crossing the high seas to Italy at their own peril.

Now, let's take a look at the powerhouse of Europe, Germany. Germany is one of the most immigrant friendly nations in Europe. Germany is a country of 83 million people. More than three million refugees and asylum seekers live there, which is more than in any other European country. Almost 300,000 people applied for asylum in Germany in 2023, the highest number since 2015, when Germany received more than one million refugees. The vast majority were from Syria followed by those from Turkey and Afghanistan. Angela Merkel, who as German chancellor at the time was praised for her open-door policy and painted as some kind of Florence Nightingale, is now criticized by her own party, the center-right Christian Democrats (the CDU) for doing what she did. A new CDU manifesto issued on December 10, 2023 pointedly replaced the phrase "Islam belongs to Germany" with wording that welcomes Muslims "who share German values."

Culture and religion are inextricably line with one another. Does that mean that Muslims will have to give up part of their religion to align with Christian values? Islam is so strict that not adhering to the most fundamental tenets of the religion can make you an apostate. And apostasy is punishable by death in Islam. This is another area of intractable friction between Muslim immigrants and German natives and another reason to stem the flow of immigrants.

Far-right politicians lament that Germany has already lost its *Leitkultur*, or "leading culture." *Leitkultur* would of course mean the majoritarian ethno-German Christian culture. And who is supposed to have overtaken that. It is Islam. A *Wall Street Journal* opinion piece claimed that "Islamic states have been recently much more successful in spreading their values to the West than vice versa."

Government statistics show that rising crime has a correlation with increasing migration. The number of criminal acts in Germany rose by about 6% in 2023 compared to 2022, with authorities attributing the increase to high levels of migration. While foreigners make up about 15% of Germany's population, they accounted for a record 41% of all crimes in 2023. Crime that authorities attributed to foreign suspects rose by 23% in 2022 and by 18% in 2023, according to government statistics. In a broad survey following European elections in 2024, personal safety was top of most voters' minds, with 74% saying they were "very worried" about a "massive" increase in crime in the future.

A recent spate of attacks hasn't helped. In June 2024, a 20-year-old German man, who was accompanying his sister after her high school graduation ball in the northwest of the country, was bludgeoned to death, allegedly by an 18-year-old Syrian. A couple of days later, a Syrian man wielding a machete triggered a melee in a small town in the southwestern state of Saarland. Soon thereafter a 24-year-old Somali allegedly stabbed another man in front of a Hamburg bar, critically injuring the victim.

But perhaps the most grievous incident occurred in Mannheim, a city in the southwestern corner of Germany. In May 2024, at an anti-Islamist rally, an Afghan man suspectedly stabbed six people, killing a police officer who had intervened who he had stabbed in the neck. Days after the death of the officer, Rouven Laur, 29, Mannheim became the reference point for a flood of anti-immigrant proposals—some once relegated to whispers only among the farthest right but that now that had moved to the center of the German political debate.

Officer Laur was charismatic and passionate about police work, according to the mayor of the small town he was from. He had taken it upon himself to learn Arabic to be able to interact better with Arabic-speaking residents, according to one of his sisters. After his death, police departments and others around the country held memorials for him. But not some Islamists. They celebrated his death with a vengeance. "Imam Meta," a hate preacher in Germany released his disturbing video calling for the death of Germans and of Muslims who don't think like him. The video was presented on Tik Tok in German.

Imam Meta's full picture is in the video. He celebrates the killing of Laur and says that the killer shall surely find the highest place in paradise and that he'll send him money, food, everything. Abhorrent, despicable, and disgusting was the reaction of the typical German politician. Platitudes all. Federal Minister of the Interior Nancy Faeser (53, SPD, social democrats) also watched the video. She was also appalled. She said: "Glorifying the murderous knife attack is disgusting and inhumane. Anyone who does this must be prosecuted with the full force of the criminal law. Our security authorities are consistently pursuing this."

So you have a police officer, Rouven Laur, who lost his life doing his duty, and an alleged Afghan killer who fill find his place in heaven according to a baleful Islamic preacher.

How many Islamists in Germany share Meta's views? Poll them, and they'll murmur condemnation. But around their dinner tables, you will find that they are either with Meta or they are saying that not what the Afghan (alleged) had done was wrong but that he was making trouble for rest of Muslims. You will have no long marches of Muslims denouncing the killer and Meta and his ilk. Pretty soon, the discourse will become one about Islamophobia. As it turned after 9/11. George W. Bush, shortly after 9/11, went to a mosque and declared that American Muslims needn't fear and that they would be protected. No attack of any major magnitude occurred in the US since 9/11, but the debate soon centered around Islamophobia, about how Muslims were being targeted.

In November 2023, with many Nazi motifs, a secret plan was hatched near Berlin not just to deport non-Germans from Germany but also all "unassimilated" German citizens. The criteria for judging assimilation was not specified, but it would have probably meant those who were not white and Christian and/or did not speak fluent German. Alliance for Democracy and CDU members were in attendance. The meeting was conducted with the utmost secrecy.

Roland Hartwig, personal aided to AfD party leader Alice Weider and an MP, was present. He is widely seen as the general-secretary of the party and claimed to represent AfD's board at the meeting. Another key person was Martin Sellner, an Austrian far-right activist, whose deportation plan it was. It is intriguing to see the influence little Austria has on big Germany. Hitler was Austrian. It is as if what Austria thinks today, Germany thinks tomorrow. And that big Germany has no problem in being led by the nose by little Austria. Austria must be one of the most right-wing countries in Europe. Having gifted the world one of the biggest monsters in history, it still doesn't shy in producing other monsters with their hate-filled invective.

An expose let to news of the secret conclave leaking out and everything that had transpired therein. So the far-right AfD and the center-right CDU were in cahoots with each other. News of the conclave led to rallies all across Germany, with more than a million people participating. The CDU kicked out its members in attendance; nothing happened to Hartwig, Weidel's aide. Now Weidel is an interesting one. She is just 49 and leads a party that is polling second in Germany, at 24%. In first place is the CDU, at 30%, which is a low for the party. The SPD (Chancellor Scholz's party) and the Greens, who together govern Germany now in a so-called traffic-light coalition, follow behind miserably and their coalition is sure to be tossed out in the next federal election in two years' time.

The AfD makes no bones about the fact that it is racist. In a hoarding displayed prominently in cities around the country, it says, "So Europe will not become Eurabia." It shows four dark-skinned Arabic men with headgear, with one of them inserting his hand inside the mouth of a naked (breasts shown clearly) white woman. It plays right into the white man's fear that blackies will carry his white woman away. It also indicates the ferocious level of licentiousness that blackies carry when compared to the soberer and subdued white man. It also shows what blackies were doing to virginal and pure Europe, denoted by the woman.

She, that is Alice Weidel, head of the AfD, is flying high. Her party has just (in June 2024) performed spectacularly in EU parliamentary elections, coming second at 16% percent of the vote. Scholz's party and its allies got a right-royal drubbing, but he has no plans to quit or call snap German federal elections. He will continue as a lame-duck chancellor, promising immigration reform but delivering little. Weidel is anything but lame-duck. In September 2024, the eastern German states of Brandenburg, Saxony and Thuringia will head to the polls; the AfD is the leading party in all three. By the next Bundestag elections, due in 2025, Weidel and her co-leader, Tino Chrupalla, could indeed be kingmakers, if not outright monarchs.

Weidel is openly lesbian. Her partner is of Sri Lankan origin. When it comes to sex, Weidel prefers dark skin, but sees red on seeing it on others. Weidel says that after Angela Merkel opened a path to ruin (by letting into Germany more than a million Syrian refugees in 2015-16), the country's current left-of-center coalition has accelerated the decline. "We'll have to see what's left of the country when they are done." No doubt she has big, ominous plans.

So there you are. Deutschland is a schizophrenic country. On the one hand, you have more than a million people participating in countrywide anti-xenophobic marches, and then you have the number one party in the country (the CDU) and the outright racist party, the AfD, collaborating. The CDU might shun an alliance with the AfD at the polls, but its sloganeering is taking much the shape of the AfD, which is the happening party defining the German landscape today. A country, Germany, that once welcomed Third World immigrants and refugees (first the Turks, and then the Syrians) is awash in wave of xenophobia where it wants to throw out every dark-skinned person, German citizen or otherwise, from its midst.

And they have a word for deportation. It's called re-migration. Shades of Nazism here. The Nazis didn't promise the Jews death. It promised them a release from their miserable existence. Some things never change. Germany is showing its Nazi face to the world. The Nazi gene is alive and kicking in Germany. The poor darkies already in Germany? Where will all of them be re-migrated to? Germany has 15% nonwhite foreigners and this doesn't include the nonwhites who have become citizens.

Do the math. 15% of 83 million (Germany's overall population) is over 12 million. Hitler sent 6 million Jews and 5 million gypsies to their death. Germany always does things, killings or re-migrations, in the millions. Spare a thought for the nonwhites living in Germany. And you thought (maybe) that immigration was a good thing! On to France now. But at this stage it must be emphasized that on no account is the author advocating that nonwhite citizens and foreigners (students, workers, illegals, asylum-seekers) be bussed out of Europe. He is just calling for a halt to fresh immigration.

Civic services in Europe are out of their depth trying tope with their own white citizens, and when you add on the load of the coloreds, that's becoming an impossible situation to handle. It breeds resentment among the white locals. That's why the far-right is on the ascendant in the Netherlands (Geert Wilder's party), in Germany (Alice Weidel's party), and in France (Marine Le Pen's party).

Wilders advocates barring students to Holland, Weidel wants to "re-migrate" all coloreds, including citizens, from Germany. Let's see what Marine Le Pen wants to do. One note on the massive anti-xenophobic million-people march held in Germany. Before the Iraq war, all of America and Europe were agog with protest marches. But once the war started, everything came down to a whimper. So do these one-off marches accomplish anything? They are fine to come out for a day, mix and mingle, and show how liberal and good you are to yourself and to your friends and family. What matters is elections, how people vote. Wilder's is the strongest party in the Dutch Parliament, Weidel is surging in Germany, and Le Pen recently came close to capturing power in France. That's what matters.

Liberte, Egalite, Fraternite are the bedrock principles of the French Republic, which means liberty, equality, and fraternity (brotherhood) for all. The "for all" is the question. If you are Zinedine Zidane, one of the greatest soccer players of all time, who is French but of Algerian descent, or Kylian Mbappe, a French soccer player widely regarded as one of the best in the world currently, who is of Cameroonian and Algerian descent, then sure you are loved, even deified in France. Zidane has been called the god of France.

In the 2022 soccer world cup, Mbappe took his team to the finals of the event, scoring a hat-trick. France lost very narrowly to Argentina, but because the way Mbappe played, France deserved to win.

French president, Emmanuel Macron, was in attendance. He kissed the sorrowful, pitiful, crying Mbappe several times on the cheek. Mbappe's sweat and tear must have entered Macron's mouth. Macron embraced Mbabbe for a full five minutes, consoling him throughout. Oh, you, who have brought glory to la belle France (the beautiful France), we love you. Macron had no hesitation in licking a black man's skin, sweat, and tears. He had no problem in rubbing his white skin against black skin. But the same Macron, in proposing a radically stringent immigration bill claimed white existential anxiety of white French people was at stake, so the bill had to be passed by the French parliament.

How do Zidane and Mbappe feel when their compatriots, the Algerians and the Cameroonians are demonized by the French president? Zidane and Mbappe have the world at their feet. They are national heroes. Beauteous white women vie to sleep with them and beget their children. Zidane is married to a gorgeous white French woman, Veronique, with whom he has four children. It's amazing that despite the racism that ordinary Algerians face from French white women, Zidane would still go for a white woman. Children born out of the wedlock of an Algerian and a white French, mixed children, face intense racism in France. Did not Zidane think for once that his mixed children would face this hostility as well? Or has he painted I am Zizou's (Zidane's nickname) child on their forehead so people would not bother them?

France is a country of 68 million. It historically has had waves of migration from Italy and Spain. But the Italians and the Spanish were white, Christian people, so assimilated easily into France. The current far-right leader, Jordan Bardella, only 28, was born to an Italian-born mother and a father of Italian and Franco-Algerian descent. His parents are considered Italian, plain and simple. As a second-generation Italian in France, he could rise to lead the National Rally, one of France's most important political parties. He doesn't even look French, he looks Italian, but that doesn't matter. As long as he's white and Christian (and of course born in France and fluent in French), he can rise to the top of French politics. Nobody in France is questioning his ethnic background.

Zidane and Mbappe too could become leading French politicians. But that is because they have brought glory to France in the country's most cherished sport of all, soccer. But, will they? Ask them. They will tell you that no matter their deity-like status is in France, and no matter how many French white women run after them, and even if they were cut out for politics and interested in it, they would not enter politics for the racism that they would face there. Historically, French presidents and prime ministers must be ethnically white. The white French man and woman likes to be ruled only by white people.

According to the French National Institute of Statistics INSEE, the 2021 census counted nearly 7 million immigrants (foreign-born people) in France, representing 10.3% of the total population. This is a decrease from INSEE statistics in 2018 in which there were 9 million immigrants (foreign-born people) in France, which at the time represented 14% of the country's total population. By 2022, the total number of new foreigners coming to France rose above 320,000 for the first time, with nearly a majority coming from Africa.

As of 2019, around 13.7 million people living in Germany, or about 17% of the population, were first-generation immigrants. So France lags behind Germany in immigration. As of the year ending June 2022, there were an estimated 10.4 people in

England and Wales who were not born in the UK. This accounts for approximately 14.8% of the total UK population. Once again France lags behind the UK.

What then explains the amount of hostility in France that even the French president is talking about white existential anxiety, which is another term, for the Great Replacement Theory, which ironically has been propounded by a French novelist, Renaud Camus. France once produced Rousseau and Voltaire and Hugo and Zola, now it's down to Renaud Camus. Having studied and worked in France, I realized how stagnant French society is. Unlike their German and English counterparts, the French, in general, do not work hard. They don't even like people who do. They might revere a Zidane or an Mbappe, but they dislike Africans (North Africans as well as Sub-Saharan West Africans) slaving in their kitchens and cleaning their rubbish. They want the food to be cooked and the country to be cleaned, but they find it odious the people (not the whites, only the nonwhites) who do them. But you can't have something cooked or cleaned if there are not people available to do the dirty work. And it's a misnomer to suggest that it's only the undocumented workers (illegal aliens) who face the rap. All coloreds do, whether they are citizens or not.

In 28 years of living in all parts of the US, not once did a cop on the street ask me for my passport. That's why I never carried my passport with anywhere I went. This of course obviated that I would lose or misplace it. Harassing colored people to show their passports and/or immigration papers is common in the EU. But in no country is it as endemic as in France. I used to take the metro every day in Paris. Unfailingly, cops would ascend my compartment and ask coloreds for their papers. *Papiers, Papiers.* I unfailingly would carry my passport on me, but so sick had I got of the whole procedure, that I didn't look at the cop, but just held aloft my visa for him to see. Very often, the cops would carry away people without papers. Goodness knows what happened to them.

Among the prominent countries in Europe, it is France where the far-right has had a long and distinguished existence, more than 50 years. The National Front was led as president by Jean-Marie Le Pen from 1972-2011 and then as honorary president from 2011-2015. He was a dedicated colored people hater, and baited Muslims and Jews, and downplayed the Holocaust. He brought his daughter, Marine Le Pen, into the National Front, but she broke with him on the subject of antisemitism to form her own party, the equally virulent National Rally. She picked Bardella to be her deputy. She aims to make Bardella the prime minister of France, while retaining the coveted post of the president of the republic for herself. Le Pen of France looks uncannily like Alice Weidel of Germany, both strong white women out to prove their testosterone. And prove her testosterone Le Pen did, winning first place in France in the EU elections held in 2023.

Shocked, Macron called for snap parliamentary elections. He didn't need to, his party was in control of parliament, but he was seeking a "clarification." And a clarification he got. In the first phase of elections in June 2024, Le Pen got a plurality of votes. But since she did not get an outright majority, a runoff was held in July. In between Macron conspired with the left, withdrawing about 200 candidates so as not to undercut each other's votes. When the results were out, the largest party was the left (but it still had not won outright majority), followed by Macron's party and then by Le Pen's. But she was not despondent. She knew she had been done in by electoral subterfuge, the kind that would not be possible in a presidential election. Le Pen has her sights set squarely on

France's presidential elections in 2027, where she will not meet Macron, because he's term-limited by his two terms in office.

To shore up his support, Macron passed a draconian anti-immigration bill in parliament. He called the left totally "immigrationiste"—a word often used by Le Pen to describe politicians who encourage uncontrolled immigration. In the past, the Le Pen, has called Mr. Macron an "immigrationiste." But after passage of Macron's immigration bill, her tone had changed. Le Penn gleefully proclaimed that she had won the battle of ideas. **She added that it was "a very small step—there is still a lot to do." Le Pen, continued, "On principle, I think it's a great ideological victory for our movement."**

French media labelled the bill as a kiss of death from Le Pen to Macron. The bill has shattered Macron's centrist image. "In 2022, after Macron was reelected president, he said, 'I won't forget all the people who voted for me because they wanted to oppose Marine Le Pen,'" said Vincent Martigny, a professor of political science at the University of Nice. "Now he's doing the opposite and paving the way for her." A leftist lawmaker, André Chassaigne, said that Macron had been elected on the promise to "protect us from the worst" of the far-right. "Today, you've gone from shield to steppingstone," Chassaigne said. Macron rejected the criticism, arguing that a lack of forceful immigration reform had fueled the far-right. Vive la France.

At the time of writing this book, which was August 2024, the UK had just sworn in a leftist Labour government of Keir Starmer. Its immigration policies and how it would implement them were unclear, so the UK, no doubt an important country, has been left out this discussion of immigration in Europe. Race riots though are sweeping the country with white hoodlums attacking and setting fire to asylum shelters with nonwhite

immigrants. Starmer is facing the challenge of his life not only in preventing the violence

but also in abating the fears of his white constituency about immigration.

5. **The Third World-ization of the First World**

At the end of World War II, European countries needed labor. Manual labor. To reconstruct themselves. Germany instituted the *gast-arbeiter* program from Turkey. South Asians didn't even need a visa to visit the UK. Nobody expected that so many denizens of the Third World would stay back in the First World.

The aim of highly-skilled workers to visit was precisely this: they would get further training and then return to their home countries to build them. Such was the case with India with renowned scientists like Homi Bhabha, who built India's nuclear program, and Vikram Sarabhai, the architect of India's famous space program. While western economies were growing, it was rare to see colored faces in any management jobs. It was expected that the Third World students who headed to the West for studies would return to their native countries upon graduation. Colored people were not welcome in white-collar jobs in the West. Yes, blue-collar workers were welcome, but even they were supposed to finish their stay and return. Colored faces in the high rungs of politics, the bureaucracy, business, media or for that matter any enterprise were simply unacceptable.

Decolonization led to a fervor in the Third World. Countries like India and China were supposed to grow rapidly, but they remained mired in mud. So the Turkish *gast-arbeiters* in Germany and the South Asians who mopped the floor at Heathrow Airport refused to go back. At least they were getting two square meals and a roof to live under in the West. If they returned to their homelands, they were not even assured of that.

Western countries "tolerated" this labor class from the East. While they were hassled by the faces that they saw, the same faces did all the dirty work that whites refused to do. And then they were not being inundated by these brown and black and yellow faces.

Strict immigration controls were rapidly being into place. Those who had got in, stayed in; those who were out were for the most part out, except in cases of chain migration, where expats pulled their families in.

Soon after their entry into the West, the Turkish and the South Asian and the African labor classes in the West started to breed. Now this posed a problem. France had the law, *jus soli,* which gave anyone born in France the right to citizenship; the law also being called birthright citizenship. Germany had no such law, but it allowed its Turkish workers to stay indefinitely in Germany and bear children. The children of the first generation of immigrants benefitted for the most part from western education. They were growing up to be doctors and lawyers and engineers and sought placement in accordance with their skills. The whites didn't like this phenomenon, and thereby racism and discrimination were born in the West. Still, laws were strict, so the second-generation skilled labor had to be accommodated in a western economy. These second-generation skilled workers were the first to shatter the glass ceiling in the West.

India and China and Africa had started growing but not rapidly enough to meet the aspirations of their people. Corruption had seeped into their leadership and systems. Indian students who decided to go to the UK to study promised their parents that they would return home but started looking for jobs in the UK after graduation. They saw the standard of life in the UK, with a house and a car being assured, and compared that to the pathetic life that they would lead in India. To tighten their belts, UK universities like Oxford and Cambridge cancelled scholarships for foreign students in the sixties, so the foreign students simply migrated to the US. Today, the UK universities regret annulling those scholarships. The UK too needed to grow, and Third World brains would certainly have helped.

Not just the poor classes, but even the middle classes in the Third World watched in envy as the sons and daughters of the labor class that had emigrated to the West prospered. The middle class started counseling their children not to come back. Forget about their children, they too wanted to make the long trek to the West. Western consulates in the Third World were inundated by visa seekers. If you had a US visa issued on your passport, you could sell the visa for a few thousand dollars in the black market. Somebody would affix their photo on the visa and change their identity and then travel to the West. Western immigration officials had wizened up, and so the first thing they would do was to scratch the photo to ascertain if it was genuinely affixed.

Third World migration to the West became a deluge in the seventies and eighties. Immigrants would return home and tell their relatives tall stories about their life in the West. Western women wore skimpy clothes and so unaccustomed Third World men thought that they were easy, and that they could bed them if they made it to the First World. Compared to the lurch they were living in, the West seemed like paradise. Immigrants didn't talk about eye-sores like racism and discrimination and the wannabe immigrants didn't want to ask.

Sometimes through chain migration, entire villages in India would migrate to the US or the UK. Yuba City is a city in California. India had ferocious anti-Sikh riots in the eighties after Sikhs massacred Hindus en masse in the Indian state of Punjab. Sikhs made a beeline for the US consulates in India. Today, Yuba City is populated mostly by Sikhs. If you are not a turbaned Sikh, you might feel out of place in Yuba City. Entire neighborhoods in the US and UK became South Asia. Germany too had its Turkish clusters, whereas in France Africans occupied the notoriously dilapidated *projets* (buildings). Former French president Nicolas Sarkozy once went to visit the *projets,* when he was serving as president, and claimed the people living there were trash and that he wanted to clean them all with a Karcher (a French pressure washing equipment).

Speaking for myself, I have spent 28 years in the US, one year in France, and visited the UK and Germany many times on extended visits. Just noting from surface appearance, the lot of nonwhite people in Anglo countries like the US and the UK is much better than that of those in France or Germany. In the US and the UK, you often see South Asians driving Rolls Royces. In fact, the joke is that if you see a Rolls Royce on the road, chances are that it is being driven by a South Asian. In France, I saw Africans mostly owning corner grocery stores, other than the Africans doing the labor work of course. In Germany, I am not so sure, but I fear that the lot of the average Turk is not so good.

Can the number of brains that migrate from the Third World to the First World turbo-charge the economy of the latter so much that it justifies their immigration? It certainly seems so. But bear in mind that white countries only let colored brains in (a) when their economies were hurting and they needed people to repair them, (b) when their economies were growing so fast that they didn't have enough people to manage the growth. It's a painful statement to make but the fundamental foundation of the world order is to maintain white dominance of the world.

So the politicians and the other powers that be in the First World welcome, for the most part, high-skilled workers from the Third World. There are exceptions to the rule of course, but it is also true that the existence of an exception tends to prove the rule. Third

World students who move to the West to study automatically become highly trained. They also assimilate into western culture much more easily. But a Geert Wilders of the Netherlands is an exception. He even wants to limit the number of students entering his country. Of course, every western country has limits on the number of students it can intake, but Wilders wants to slash the already existing limit in his country. Perhaps because the Netherlands is a small, crowded country or may be because Wilders is too much of an extremist.

My father was visiting the US in 1990. My brother and his Indian roommate were doing their MBAs from the University of Chicago. My father asked them what they were contributing to the US. Stumped at first, they answered they were creating and giving jobs. I don't know what happened to my brother's roommate, but my brother founded an internet company that went public and now employs about 800 people. So he was proven right. He did create and give jobs. But Third World skilled migrants are driven to succeed. Often it's a case of besting the whites. It's a great honor for them if they become CEOs and leaders in other fields like medicine and academia.

It's a well-known fact that no matter how successful a Third World migrant is in the West, he or she never breaks their umbilical cord to their home countries. They are always worried what their home countries think of them. If they are successful in the West, they are splashed everywhere in their native lands. This pleases them enormously. To get the approbation of their native lands is what, in part, imbues in them such a ferocious drive in the West. They have sons and daughters of their own and quite often they want them to marry people from their homelands. The bigger the reputation that they have, the better their chances of attracting quality brides and grooms for their children.

Now think about this for a minute. Western countries pride themselves on being meritocracies, which in many instances they are. But when faced with ferocious drive from nonwhite immigrants, western people, both white and colored, wither away. In the US, I cannot think of a significant company that was founded by a first-generation immigrant. Google's CEO is Indian and so is YouTube's (YouTube is part of Google) but Google was founded by Americans (Sergey Brin, one of the two co-founders, was born in Moscow but immigrated from the Soviet Union to the US at the age of six, so one can posit that he was raised in the US for the most part and that practically he was a second-generation immigrant and not a first-generation one).

There are any number of significant companies like Google. Facebook. Microsoft. Amazon. All founded by Americans but which employ a lot of first-generation Indians in key roles. What does that tell you? That Americans are good in ideation, transforming those ideas into systems, and then growing those systems into valuable businesses. They then are open enough to hire the best and the brightest from first-generation immigrants to lead their companies. What is the other thing that it tells you? That the first-generation is not ready to ideate and build successful companies of their own. By successful companies here, I mean the Googles and the Microsofts, companies that have scaled to tens of thousands of employees, and not my brother's company, which is too small when compared with the Googles and the Microsofts.

Every first-generation immigrant who becomes the CEO of a western company takes that job away from a western person because the first-generation person is deemed more qualified by his or her mostly western colleagues. This is the essence of western meritocracy, to reward the brightest and the best. But think of India and China, both well-doing economies with any number of significant companies, but how many are open enough to hire foreigners to lead them? Take the case of Air India, India's flagship carrier. Air India got privatized and wanted a Turkish man to lead them.

But relations between India and Turkey were frayed. So the ruling political party objected to a Turk taking the helm of Air India, which rescinded his appointment.

Can you think of such a thing happening in the States? For sure not. Uber's CEO, Dara Khosrowshahi, immigrated from Iran to the US when he was 12. Hostile relations between Iran and the US did not prevent Uber from appointing him CEO. China and the US too are not on the best of terms, but I doubt that the US government will interfere if a big American company wants to appoint a first-generation Chinese as its CEO. But letting in single-minded-to-succeed immigrants also puts pressure on natives, whether it is at school or at work. In Silicon Valley, where I have lived for nearly two decades, Asian and East Indian parents themselves are driven, but they drive their own wards to so much distraction that white children cannot keep up. Then the best universities like Stanford and University of California at Berkeley are swamped with Asian and East Indian students, breeding resentment amongst the native whites and blacks. The book, *Battle Hymn of the Tiger Mother*, by Amy Chua, who herself is a professor at Yale Law School and who was born to Chinese-Filipino parents, is an interesting study.

Chua employs the term "Tiger Mother" to describe a mother who is a strict disciplinarian. Chua reported that in one study of 48 Chinese immigrant mothers, the vast majority "said that they believe their children can be 'the best' students, the notion is paramount that 'academic achievement reflects successful parenting,' and that if children did not excel in school, then there was 'a problem' in the household and the parents 'were not doing their job.'" Chua contrasts them with the view she labels "Western"–that a child's self-esteem is most important. Such attitudes are commonly found in other Asian parents, specifically East Indian parents, living in the West.

Whites and blacks have been relentless in building America and taking it to the top, economically and militarily, but is a single-minded immigrant drive healthy for American culture, a culture that may not have seen something like this before. Many American kids just give up in the face of this passion and accept their status as second-class B-graders. The passion extends into the workforce as well. The average American works his 8 hours a day, more or less, and then does other things. Many Asians and East Indians work far harder, pulling in nights and weekends. Of course then they are going to outperform the whites in their jobs and gain a better chance of being promoted over them.

Some Asians and East Indians maintain that it is not they who want to work such long hours. They blame systemic discrimination. They claim that if they did not work extremely long hours, they would not survive in a white workplace, that the very reason that they are hired in the first place is because they are expected to slog. If they were to revert to a white work routine, they would be fired. Now there could be some truth in their belief. HR and company management and senior staff might want workaholics, but the average white colleague, who finds it unbearable to work extended hours and especially those for free, might be repulsed by the presence of Asians and East Indians.

While Indians celebrate the fact that so many political and business leaders in the West, especially in the US, are of Indian descent, many ordinary whites and blacks on the other hand might feel resentment. Whites feel that the West is being taken over by brown people and that they have to take orders from colored people. Blacks have a feeling of despair, of being completely left behind. They were having a hard time keeping up with the whites when the US was a white world. Now they have a chance in hell. Social networks in school, college and the workplace also tend to be parochial, so a group identity—both a self-identity as well as how you are perceived by other people—develops. Mixing of ethnicities is not as common as believed. America has ceased to remain a melting pot.

We have talked about high-skilled workers migrating to the West and about the impact this migration has on the society there. But the brain migrants from the Third World are far outnumbered by the brawn migrants. The Indian prime minister, Narendra Modi, was in Austria in July 2024. India is a giant country of 1.4 billion. Austria is a tiny country of 9 million. In Austria, Modi asked for more work visas for Indians. The Austrians said that they would consider his request.

How strange this is. The most populous country in the world asking one of the tiniest countries in the world for work visas for its population. Austria too has unemployment and is probably growing at the First World average of 1-3%. India is growing at 7%, but the Indian prime minister feels compelled to send his people to all parts of the First World.

Wherever Modi goes in the First World, he asks for more student and work visas. Western countries are not so much interested in the unskilled labor now. They already have enough of immigrants and locals to do the menial work, the grunt work. European countries have seen the success that hi-tech workers from India have brought to the United States and want to emulate that success. Germany, in fact, started a "green card" scheme on the pattern of the US green card (permanent residency) to attract high-tech workers. It took off to a slow start, but seems to be now attracting more and more Indian techies. Modi became prime minister of India in 2014. In his first Independence Day speech, he exhorted his people to control their population.

That plea fell on deaf years. Indians are obsessed with having babies. And then, historically, a previous government had enforced population control so rabidly that it became a political hot potato. No government since then wants to talk about limiting India's population explosion. Modi has been prime minister since 2014 and has given nine more Independence Day speeches. Not ever again has he brought up the subject of population control.

Instead the Indian government has settled on a new formula. Export as much uneducated labor to the First World as well as to the Gulf countries to control its population, reduce poverty, and receive remittances from the emigres. In 2022-23, India earned a healthy $108 billion in remittances from abroad. India's total exports (merchandise and services) in 2023-24 were $778 billion. You can see how that remittances from the Indian diaspora abroad are a healthy when compared to its overall exports. And in receiving remittances, the Indian government has to do nothing. Indian workers labor abroad and send money to the country, to primarily their families. In exports, people in India have to do real work and the government has to produce a conducive atmosphere and policies for industry and agriculture to grow.

The Indian government has decided to take a short cut: Offer its labor as a human resource to much of the world. The Indian diaspora is close to 30 million strong. There are 193 member states of the UN. A study showed that there was at least one person of Indian origin present in 191 states of the lot. That is how dispersed the Indian diaspora is.

The educated emigres from India at least have received good education in English, in STEM subjects and are fairly westernized in their behavior and mannerisms. The uneducated Indian labor class is not. Many of them go straight from their village to the First World.

Gandhi said that India lived in its villages. India still lives in it villages. But rural distress is omnipresent in India and scarcely any Indian government has done much to address the matter. Rural India is rife with unemployment and disease and illiteracy. Industry is very scarce in rural India partly because city-slick Indian industrialists do not want to live in the villages. Disease is rampant because sanitation and hygiene are poor. If the government has set up any hospital, it is too remote or doesn't work at all. Doctors do not want to be posted to rural areas. And the less said about rural government schools, the better.

If the culture shock on coming to the West for an educated India is great, then the same for an uneducated labor-class Indian is manifold times higher. I have come across labor class Indians on the verge of suicide on coming to the West. They cannot turn back and go to India. In many cases they don't have the money to pay the return fare. And the ignominy that they would face in their village would be stinging. In the West, they are lost completely. They barely speak English, not even enough to get by in the US or the UK. If they migrate to Germany, their knowledge of German is nil. The same is the case with every other European country. They try to converse in their pidgin English to the locals, but the locals seeing how shabby they are, only talk to them in their native language.

The labor class from the Third World then sticks to its own kind. They might interact with some locals at work and pick up a few words of the local language here and there, but in their personal sphere, they rest content with their countrymen, in fact with people who speak the same mother tongue that they do and those that belong to their own religion. This tendency to cluster together is not just present in the labor classes; the educated immigrant in the West practices it too to the hilt.

In India, men tend to urinate in the open. Public stalls are so filthy, that an open-air leak is much preferred. This habit cuts across all classes. If you are driving from say Delhi to Mumbai, and you don't come across a rest stop anywhere, people will just stop along the road and urinate. This habit is inculcated in elders as well as youngsters. Boys see their fathers doing it at will, so follow the leader. My friend was doing his MBA from The University of Chicago. He took off on a road trip. He badly felt the pressure, so stooped his car along the highway and unzipped his pants. Before he knew it, a cop was tapping him on the shoulder. He issued him a $200 ticket. My friend pleaded, I am from India, this habit is very common there, please don't give me a ticket. Remorselessly, the cop replied, this is not India. The ticket will serve as a good lesson for you for the future. I don't know if my friend gave up his habit or not.

So there are many mannerisms common to the First World that are absent in the Third World. Holding doors open. Keeping lift doors ajar for people, not spitting on the street, no open defecation, depositing trash in bins, picking up after your pets, these are all practices common in the West. Educated classes in the Third World practice the opposite with gay abandon, leave alone the illiterate people from the villages. In India, women generally wear much less skimpy clothes than women in the West. Many Indians when they arrive in the West for the first time equate the morals of western women with the amount of clothes they wear: If they are scantily dressed, they must be easy.

My neighbor, a 94-year old Indian Lothario, went to visit his son in LA. He told me, by gosh, the women here are overtly friendly. They wear skimpy clothes that show off their breasts and legs, and are constantly smiling at me with come-hither glances and how do you do. I lived in the US and was having trouble finding a girlfriend at that time. I laughed at my neighbor and said that American women are like that. They are friendly on the surface, but dare you make a pass at them, and you will know what rejection means. My neighbor still didn't believe me. He thought I was a loser in that I was not able to snag a girl in America. I am sure he must have tried his outreach to some women but he is not one to talk about failed exploits, nor did I press him to disclose anything.

Rudyard Kipling wrote, *Oh, East is East, and West is West, and never the twain shall meet, Till Earth and Sky stand presently at God's great Judgement Seat;*

The emigration of Third World people to the West is really a collision of two cultures very different from each other. Some eastern men marry western women, and try to cloak them in burqas, change their religion, customs, dietary habits, etc. This transformation of their women is watched with much consternation by many natives. They feel that eastern people in the West should adapt to western ways and thereby assimilate in the West. They are wary of alien sub-cultures sprouting in their lands. Because people from the Third World in general procreate faster than their western counterparts, Westerners are wary that their civilizations will soon become Eurabia or Euafrica or Englishstan.

There is another problem with the mass migration of uneducated Third World people to the West. Because their education and IQ levels tend to be low, they lower the overall education and IQ levels of western societies. Many of them do not speak the native language and have a hard time transmitting it to their children. They struggle to help children with their homework. This is what I call the Third World-ization of the First World.

Alice Weidel, head of the hard-right Alternative for Democracy party in Germany faults immigrants for Germany's poor showing in a recent PISA study comparing education across countries. "The level is automatically reduced if they come from a non-[German]-linguistic, non-[German]-cultural and educationally uneducated context," she says. She has a point. Foreigners do make up a growing proportion of schoolchildren in Germany, and tend to score lower than native Germans in tests. (PISA is the OECD's Program for International Student Assessment, PISA measures 15-year-olds' ability of their reading, mathematics, and science knowledge and skills to meet real-life challenges.)

So there you are, First World. Immigrate Third World labor classes at your own peril. Your own people used to do the so-called menial work before the immigrants arrived but now don't want to do it anymore. It is not if your uneducated classes are bettering themselves by gaining more education. Many of them are lazing about and on welfare. Immigrants in the UK score higher than native-born Britons in the same PISA study. This could be because immigrants in the UK are generally South Asian, who value education much more than immigrants in Germany, who tend be Turkish and Syrian and Afghan. Native-born westerners have to relearn how to get their hands dirty back again doing low-class work, otherwise the West will stay inundated with Third World refugees, asylum-seekers, and other immigrants.

6. **The Great Replacement Theory Aka The white genocide conspiracy theory**

Let's consider a book with a far-fetched idea: ONE BILLION AMERICANS. The Case for Thinking Bigger. By Matthew Yglesias. Yglesias worked for the ultra-liberal think tank, the Center for American Progress from 2008-11. Yglesias's liberal credentials are thus clear. There are **about 330 million Americans right now**, which means that getting to one billion would mean adding 670 million net new humans.

One way that Yglesias intends to meet his goal is through immigration. But he's pragmatic about it. He's happy to assuage xenophobes by being open to fairly unrestricted immigration from "Canada, Australia, the Anglophone Caribbean, America's NATO allies or some other subset of countries that seems popular." Think of it for a second. Most of his immigrant choices are from white countries. Canada and Australia already need immigration to grow and have low populations. How the hell are they going to meet Yglesias's goal?

Consider the Anglophone Caribbean. I presume that means black Caribbean folk whose mother tongue is English. Why not include Indians then? Everybody knows that about a 100 million Indians speak better English than the English themselves. Or are they left out because they are Hindu and the Anglophone Caribbean are in because they are Christian? So Yglesias, himself of Jewish background, wants white or black people in as long as their first language is English. All this stuff from the mind of a liberal. Now wait till you hear about what I have got for you.

 Renaud Camus (not to be mistaken for Albert Camus, who won the Nobel Prize in Literature) is a French novelist and sometime politician. **He is the inventor of the "Great Replacement," a white nationalist, far-right conspiracy theory** that states that, with the complicity or cooperation of "global replacist" elites, the ethnic French and white European populations at large are being demographically and culturally replaced by nonwhite peoples—especially from Muslim-majority countries—through mass migration, demographic growth of the migrants and a drop in the birth rate of white Europeans. One can add the US and Canada and Australia and New Zealand to the mix of countries affected so. But, who are these "global replacist" elites? Camus doesn't specify but he probably means leftist politicians and wealthy financiers like George Soros. But if you look at France, three of the last five presidents—Chirac, Sarkozy, and Macron—have come from the right. Mitterrand and Hollande were socialist. The power elite in France should be therefore somewhat equally divided between liberal and conservative. But no, Camus brings up this "imaginary" power elite which is clandestinely colluding with immigrant cartels and émigré countries to somehow turn his beloved France black, brown, and yellow.

Camus is gay. The antecedent of his great replacement theory is the white genocide conspiracy theory, which says that Jews will replace white Christian people around the world. Now let's consider the West for an instant. America has about 200 million white Christians and the EU another 400 million. That is 600 million people will need to be replaced. Jews are in minuscule numbers around the world. How do you expect them to replace anybody, leave alone more than half a billion white Christians? Camus was clever. It's not fashionable to blame the Jews for everything, is it? We know what happened in the last century. Nobody, even the alt-right, wants that to repeat that. Plus, many of the Jews are white. White people replacing white people? Doesn't sound right.

White genocide sounds odious. He gave it a new name, Great Replacement, and with a new target, Muslims instead of Jews. Now there are 1.8 billion Muslims in the world. They could easily overrun 600 million white Europeans. Great replacement is a better dog whistle than white genocide. The dog—extreme xenophobia—is still a Rottweiler, but the whistle has changed. The Ku Klux Klan members demonstrating in Charlottesville, Virginia in 2017 carried placards that read, You will not replace us, and Jews will not replace us.

Who was the "you" in the first set of placards? It obviously meant Jews. Then why have two separate placards? Camus said that he didn't approve of Nazis or violence, but could understand why white Americans felt angry about being replaced, and that he approved of the sentiment. The Klan members in Charlottesville coopted his replacement theory and replaced his nemesis—Muslims—with their nemesis du jour—Jews. ("Du jour" because the Klan in America goes after Muslims too.) Now by replacing Muslims by Jews, it sounded fair and lovely. Numerous terror incidents have come about in the world that have had Camus's great replacement theory as an inspiration.

Each time Camus has distanced himself from the violence. But his own fear of Muslims is based on violence. Muslims will overrun white Christians, he says. It's going to be an invasion, he says. One way he says that Muslims will replace whites is because they breed much faster. Or, they will kill or convert. Aha, "kill." There you have violence. Muslim men will "groom" white women and miscegenate with them and procreate colored, Muslim offspring. No time frame is attached to when all of this might happen. No numbers are cited. Camus just says the he lived in the French countryside for a while and saw the ethnic composition of the villages change, so that's how he came up with the idea for Great Replacement.

There is something about Great Replacement that incites violence, in a way that the white genocide theory doesn't do. The following are some of the recorded violent events when Great Replacement has come into play. In October 2018, a gunman killed 11 people and injured 6 in an attack on the Tree of Life synagogue in Pittsburgh, Pennsylvania. The gunman believed Jews were deliberately importing nonwhite immigrants into the United States as part of a conspiracy against the white race. Bear in mind though that in Camus's worldview it is not Jews but the Muslims who are the guilty party

Brenton Harrison Tarrant, the Australian terrorist responsible for the mass shootings at Al Noor Mosque and Linwood Islamic Centre in Christchurch, New Zealand, on March 15, 2019, that killed 51 people and injured 49, named his manifesto *The Great Replacement*, a reference to Camus's book. In response, Camus condemned violence while reaffirming his desire for a "counter-revolt" against an increase in nonwhite populations. In 2019, research by the Institute for Strategic Dialogue showed over 24,000 social media mentions of the Great Replacement in the month before the Christchurch shootings, in comparison to just 3,431 mentions in April 2012. The use of the term spiked in April 2019 after the Christchurch mosque shootings.

Patrick Crusius, the suspect in the 2019 El Paso, Texas shooting, shot dead 23 Latinos in the deadliest attack on Latinos in modern American history. He posted an online manifesto titled *The Inconvenient Truth* alluding to the "great replacement" and expressing support for "the Christchurch shooter" minutes before his attack. The manifesto spoke of a "Hispanic invasion of Texas" leading to "cultural and ethnic replacement" (alluding to the *Reconquista*) as justifications for the shooting.

The suspect accused in the 2022 Buffalo shooting, in which 10 African-Americans were murdered, listed the Great Replacement in a manifesto he had published prior to the attack. The suspect described himself as a fascist, white supremacist, and anti-Semite. So we see here as in the Charlottesville violence and the attack on the synagogue in Pittsburgh that anti-Semites have coopted Camus's Great Replacement theory. It is not only terrorists that have been inspired by Great Replacement, but presidents and prominent TV personalities as well.

 According to the Institute for Strategic Dialogue, Donald Trump has referenced the Great Replacement, and a 2019 tweet in favor of his proposed Border Wall was interpreted by many as endorsing the theory. They also stated that Trump's Twitter account was one of the most influential accounts promoting the theory. His history of describing Muslims and immigrants as "invaders," according to SBS News, closely mirrors the language of explicit supporters of the theory. Political scientist Robert A. Pape concluded from two surveys led by the Chicago Project on Security and Threats in 2021 that the Great Replacement theory had achieved "iconic status with white nationalists" and "might help explain why such a high percentage of the rioters involved in the January 6 United States Capitol attack hailed from counties with fast-rising, nonwhite populations."

In mid-September 2021, the U.S. media turned its attention to an increasing number of Haitian migrants seeking protection at the border in Del Rio, Texas. Some Haitian families were allowed to stay in the US and pursue asylum claims in immigration court. On Sept. 22, cable television host Tucker Carlson provided his own theory as to what was happening at the border. In a segment entitled "Nothing About What's Happening Is an Accident," Carlson said that current U.S. border policy is designed to "change the racial mix of the country. ... In political terms this policy is called the 'great replacement,' the replacement of legacy Americans with more obedient people from faraway countries." Carlson concluded that President Biden's policies with regard to the Haitian migrants have put the U.S. on a "suicidal" path. Since Carlson's comments, numerous public figures on the far-right have echoed or supported the Great Replacement theory.

According to a *New York Times* analysis published in April 2022, Carlson has made reference to the theory in more than 400 episodes between 2016 and 2021. Donald Trump considered Carlson as his VP pick for the 2020 presidential elections. Carlson is incredibly popular in alt-right circles. No matter what happens to the political fortunes of Trump, Carlson has a bright future in the Republican Party if he chooses to go into politics.

Let's ignore the uneducated migrants for a second. Say you are an Indian software engineer based in the US or in Germany. After a hard day's work, you have come home to relax with your family. The Great Replacement theory has gone mainstream in the West. So you see a Tucker Carlson (or his counterpart in Germany) berating nonwhite immigrants for taking jobs away from whites. They refer to Indian immigrants as an invasion. Indian prime minister, Narendra Modi, refers to Muslims in India as "infiltrators," even though the overwhelming majority of Muslims in India have lived in the country for centuries. For his expression, Modi is pilloried in western media.

But as Christ said, when you point a finger at someone, three fingers point back at you. Those three fingers are pointing back at the West. Trump, Carlson, New Gingrich, Matt Gaetz, JD Vance, Vivek Ramaswamy, and Elise Stefanik are among a large number of prominent American personalities who have endorsed the Great Replacement. So the software engineer who has come back home for the night switches the Carlson channel off but finds that on every other channel immigration is the hot topic du jour. He goes to sleep disturbed. Not only disturbed for himself and his spouse, but for his children who will grow up in the West but look Indian. Then their children would meet the same fate of being made to feel unwanted.

If you think that this is a far cry, then look only at the Turkish population in Germany. Even into its third or fourth generations, they have not been able to obtain German nationality. Forget a piece of paper. They are treated as outcastes for the color of their skin and their Muslim religion, even though they speak fluent German. In February 2000, the German computer association BITKOM asked the German government to allow the entry of up to 30,000 foreign professionals to help fill what BITKOM said were 75,000 vacant jobs for computer programmers. Then-Chancellor Gerhard Schroeder responded positively, proposing what he called a "green card" program that would allow non-EU foreigners to enter Germany for up to five years. The green card program, it was hoped, would help to highlight the benefits of foreigners. The opposition made opposition to green cards the centerpiece of its hate campaign in a state election, using the slogan *"Kinder statt Inder"* (children instead of Indians) to argue that Germans should have more children and train them instead of importing high-tech workers from India.

The Indian economy is experiencing a rapid year-over-year growth of about 7%, but with population growth outpacing economic growth, there are not many jobs available. Figures for unemployment are unreliable. Many studies just focus on the middle- and upper-classes, ignoring the vast amount of poor in their calculations. Just in the general elections of 2024, Priyanka Gandhi, a prominent opposition politician repeatedly claimed that 700 million youth in the country were unemployed. The ruling party of Prime Minister Narendra Modi did not come up with a counter to that. That means that even the powers that be know the true state of unemployment in the country.

Discrimination against Muslims in India and their lynching by Hindu mobs is a common occurrence. I was just reading an article by the Indian journalist, Rana Ayyub, in the *Washington Post*, entitled Where lynchings still happen. The answer: India and Pakistan. The lynchings in India are those of Muslims by Hindus; in Pakistan those by Muslims of Hindus and Christians and minority Muslim sects. A Muslim in the Gujarat state of India, from where Modi hails, and which has become rabidly-anti-Muslim, was beaten to death by a 5,000 strong Hindu mob for doing well in a cricket match. The Hindus could not stomach a Muslim beating Hindus at a game.

Uttar Pradesh is India's largest state. It can also be the most unsafe for Muslims, since it is ruled by a rapid Hindu preacher, Yogi Adityanath, who bulldozes Muslim properties with impunity, thereby earning the moniker of "Bulldozer Baba." Frighteningly, he is in line to become India's prime minister one day. Uttar Pradesh is one of 20 out of 28 states in India where there is a ban on cow slaughter and the sale of cows. But many Muslims are farmers who have to herd their cattle on the road, transporting them to fresh pastures.

Tens of lynchings of such farmers have been reported, with Hindu mobs assaulting them for being cattle traffickers.

What does it mean to be Muslim in India? A life of fear and agony. Many Muslims thereby want to migrate to Canada and other countries in the West. At least their livelihood will be protected there. But are they sure about that? Right now (August 2024), the UK is ablaze because the hard-right is out to kill asylum seekers. The rioters believe that an asylum seeker killed three girls in Southport. They are wrong. It was a British 17-year old youth born in Cardiff, Wales. His name is Alex Rudakubana. By his first name he sounds Caucasian and his last name doesn't sound Muslim, but the suspect is black. Rioters have set a Holiday Inn in Rotherham, Yorkshire on fire where are a number of terrified Muslim asylum seekers have sought refuge. Liverpool, which is 20 miles south of Southport, is ablaze with rioting.

One hard-right British woman said that the asylum seekers were doing to the whites in the UK what the whites had done to the Native Americans in America: "they are pushing us out." Another man claimed that immigration to the UK was at a boiling point. Is this the life that asylum-seekers in the Third World aspire to as they make their way to the West? First, there is the treacherous journey, then this frightful welcome, and then a life of drudgery akin to slavery. Weren't they better in their own homelands? No, in their mind at least, the homeland ridden by crime and poverty and murder was even worse. When Angela Merkel allowed over a million refugees mainly from Syria into Germany in 2015-16, many Germans welcomed them with open arms. But neo-Nazi hoodlums also torched many Syrian shelters with firebombs. It seems like the Nazi gene has never really left Germany.

James Byrd Jr., an African American man was murdered by three white men, two of whom were avowed white supremacists, in Jasper, Texas, on June 7, 1998. Shawn Berry, Lawrence Brewer, and John King dragged Byrd for three miles (five kilometers) behind a Ford pickup truck along an asphalt road. Byrd, who remained conscious for much of his ordeal, was killed about halfway through the dragging when his body hit the edge of a culvert, severing his right arm and head. The murderers drove on for another 1.5 miles (2.5 kilometers) before dumping his torso in front of a Black church. Jasper is in east Texas.

I moved to Austin, Texas to work in early 1999. Austin is quite far from east Texas where Jasper is located, but for me, a stranger, Texas was still Texas. At that time, most roads in Austin didn't have sidewalks. You either walked on the embankment or on the divider. I didn't have a car then and walked 3 miles from my hotel to work. I was always terrified if somebody would pump a few bullets into me as I walked on the road. One Thanksgiving, I decided to go to New Orleans. I had to drive through east Texas as I made my way to New Orleans. Terrified as I was, I didn't stop even at a rest stop until I had crossed east Texas. The following year, my father visited me in Austin. I took him to New Orleans. He desperately wanted a cup of tea while we were in east Texas. We stopped at a McDonald's, I barged in, got a cup of tea for him, and scrammed from that place as fast as I could. I didn't tell my father anything about the Jasper incident.

Discrimination, prejudice, and constant barbs that you as an immigrant are taking jobs from locals, are the lot of nonwhite immigrants in the West. Right now (August 2024), mosques and Muslim shops are under attack in the UK. If a hard-right mob comes across a Muslim man on the street, they will quarter him, tear him from limb to limb. Every other month, an Indian or two are shot dead by white nationalists in the US. Sometimes

the nationalists think that the Indians are Iranians, so they have a triple hatred towards

them for being nonwhite, Muslim, and Iranian (because Iran is an enemy of the US). But

in hardly any instance do the families of the victims want to go back to India. They

continue singing hosannas to the US. Educated Indians might have a better life in the US

than in India, but if you discount racism, discrimination, and the odd physical assault, is

their life really better in the US?

On August 5, 2012, a gunman, Wade Michael Page, who had ties to white supremacist

organizations, entered the Oak Creek, Wisconsin, gurdwara, a Sikh house of worship, and

fatally shot seven congregants. All of the victims were residing legally in the US. One of

the victims was a woman. The Sikhs wear turbans, not too dissimilar from what Bin

Laden used to wear. Maybe Page mistook the Sikhs for Arabs. But perhaps maybe not.

He was just out to kill Sikhs, nonwhite foreigners in his eyes. The gurdwara issued a

statement after the killing pledging allegiance to the US. So this is it. Despite their people

being shot or lynched from limb to limb or firebombed and their places of worship

desecrated and their businesses and residences looted and vandalized, nonwhite

immigrants still don't want to leave western countries that have caused them so much

harm.

This then is the effect of Great Replacement, white genocide conspiracy theory, or white

extinction anxiety, or whatever else you want to call it. White nationalist thugs are on the

rampage against nonwhite immigrants, legal and illegal, and western countries are just

taking the violence in their stride by not instituting effective control, etc. Not only the

powers that be in the countries, but even the victimized communities and the relatives of those killed cling on to live in the same western country that at times has proven so tortuous to them. They still refuse to return to their homelands. Perhaps it will take the extinction of nonwhite immigrants on a mass scale for that to happen. In any case, one extinction anxiety, white, is colliding with another extinction anxiety, that of nonwhite immigrants. Who will triumph is anybody's guess. With so much hatred prevailing in western countries, does it make sense to have large-scale nonwhite immigration to them?

7. **Will America have a foreign-born non-US parent US citizen as president?**

It was the summer of 1990. Ours was a new contingent of Indian graduate students attending Purdue University at West Lafayette, Indiana. Jaishree was a pretty girl in our group and quite worldly-wise. We Indians felt strange in a foreign land and tended to stick together. We noticed that African Americans were quite well acculturated to America, and some even seemed to get along well with whites. Jaishree remarked, Oh, but they are their own after all. Who are we? Just a bunch of foreigners, alluding to the fact the blacks were after all part of white America.

The US Constitution insists that the president must be a "natural born" citizen of the US. What natural born has come to mean today will be discussed later in the chapter. There was some confusion that the president had to be born in the US. This led to the "birther" conspiracy instigated by Donald Trump against Barack Obama. Trump insisted that Obama was not born in the US and was therefore disqualified from becoming US president. Trump's assertion was only dispelled when Obama showed his birth certificate, both the short form and the long form, clearly highlighting that he was born in Hawaii. Obama was born to a white American woman and an immigrant father from Kenya. Few felt that Obama had a chance to become president. Was the US ready for its first black president or even "mixed" president, as the French would say?

Obama's good looks, his highfalutin oratory, and the mess that his predecessor, George W. Bush, had left behind, catapulted him to the White House. There, he and his wife Michelle, who too is black, realized what a novel experience they were for the nation and tried to hide their blackness as much as possible. Obama played golf mostly with white men. It was only when, in the aftermath of the Charleston church shooting by a white supremacist of ten African Americans, Obama visited the church that he let his full black self go and sang Amazing Grace with amazing grace.

People felt that Obama had broken a big glass ceiling by becoming the first African American to become president, but such was not precisely the case. Donald Trump, who followed him, was a demagogue who stirred up white extinction anxiety and referenced the Great Replacement in his speeches. It seemed that white America had revolted against a black man in the White House, and just wanted to put back the white in the White House.

Trump almost destroyed America to fulfill his self-serving needs and in came Joe Biden. Biden is prone to gaffes, and he has made the off racist comment at times. For instance, he has said that you cannot go to a 7-Eleven or a Dunkin' Donuts unless you have a slight Indian accent. Biden meant that these stores employed mostly Indians, and the Indian crew would not understand a pure American accent. Biden tried to paper over the comment, but it didn't work.

But Biden has arguably done more for African Americans since Lyndon B. Johnson passed the civil rights bill. He quietened the black lives matter movement, chose a black woman as his running mate, sent a black woman to the Supreme Court, and appointed black people at many levels in his administration, including in his Cabinet. Biden by his actions has proven that he is not racist. He was willing to hand over the keys to the Ferrari to a black woman, which he eventually did.

Kamala Harris is an interesting mix of West Indian (her father was Jamaican) and East Indian (her mother was Indian). In Harris's case, the east quite literally met the west, rebuffing Kipling. But the person who has been responsible for her becoming the

Democratic nominee for president is not Barack Obama but Joe Biden. Obama and his wife, Michelle, were one of the last few eminent people to endorse Harris for president. In 2016, Obama dissuaded Biden from running, preferring to put his weight behind Hillary Clinton, with disastrous results. It is all for the good for Harris that Biden didn't run in 2016. He might have seen her as too inexperienced to be picked as his VP candidate then. She was the attorney-general of California in 2016, and only in the November 2016 election did she win a seat in the upper house. She was sworn in as US senator in 2017. Becoming a senator added gravitas to her resume and made her catch Biden's eye.

Now Harris is running for president. If she wins, she'll be the first woman to become president, the first black woman to become president, and the first person of East Indian descent to become president. Donald Trump, her opponent is trying to paint her as alien by playing with her first name. Her first name is pronounced Comma-la or even better, Camma-la. Trump mangles her as Kamaala, Kamabla, Camilla and whatnot. He tried to do the same with Barack Obama, paying a lot of stress to his middle name, Hussein, to prove that Obama was Muslim. He succeeded with that with his MAGA (Make America Great Again) crowd and won the presidency in 2016.

Until now, Trump has not mocked Harris's middle name, which is Devi and which means goddess in Indian. But wait and watch. He might start doing so to paint her as some kind of pagan Hindu idol. Idolatory as you know is banned in Protestantism but not so much in Catholicism, what with images of Jesus and Mary. Most of white America is Protestant, but Harris is Protestant too, so we'll see how it goes. Trump is definitely gunning for Harris's race. He says she was Indian until she turned black to appease voters. Harris's

Indian mother, Shyama Gopalan, determinedly believed that Harris and her sister Maya would be considered as black in America so took them to a black church to pray as well as to Sunday school. Harris and Maya were brought up Protestant. It is unclear if Shyama Gopalan ever converted to Protestantism.

Harris went to a historically black university, Howard, and has always identified herself as black, even though she never shies away from her Indian, and especially South Indian, roots. In a cooking session with the Indian-American actress Mindy Kaling, Kaling asks Harris if she was Indian, and Harris vigorously nods her head yes. This is the video that perhaps that Donald is referring too. He himself is of German and Irish descent, but wrongfully claimed Swedish ancestry. This is what America has become—a melting pot of races and ethnicities.

Obama and Harris are all second-generation immigrants, born in the US. According to the Constitution: "No Person except a natural born Citizen, or a Citizen of the United States, at the time of the Adoption of this Constitution, shall be eligible to the Office of President; neither shall any Person be eligible to that Office who shall not have attained to the Age of thirty-five Years, and been fourteen Years a Resident within the United States." One of the reasons why the framers of the Constitution made natural-born citizenship a requirement of being the president was to explicitly show allegiance to America. (The first nine presidents and the twelfth president, Zachary Taylor, were all citizens at the adoption of the Constitution in 1789, with all being born within the territory held by the United States and recognized in the Treaty of Paris. All other presidents who have served were born in the United States and after 1789.)

But what happens if a natural-born citizen of America takes a second citizenship—say that of the UK or any other country that allows dual citizenship. (America for its part does). Now can the dual-citizenship holder still run for president or will he by law have to drop his second citizenship? I see nowhere that requirement. Secondly if a man takes a second citizenship, isn't he showing more loyalty to that country than to the United States?

Countries like India do not allow dual citizenship. So if you are Indian, as I am, and you become a naturalized American citizen, as I have done, you have to forego your Indian citizenship and just be American.

One strong proponent of a first-generation immigrant becoming the president of the United States is the former governor of California, Arnold Schwarzenegger. Schwarzenegger was born in Austria and became a naturalized American citizen. He was not barred from holding the office of the governor of California but cannot become president even though he has expressed the desire to so by amending the Constitution. If Schwarzenegger runs for president, he will be taken seriously as a candidate. I asked my friend Julia, a white blonde from upstate Michigan, is she would accept a foreign-born naturalized citizen of America as president. She emphatically said no. She said she wouldn't know where that person's loyalties would lie, with America, or say in the case of Schwarzenegger, with Austria.

As more and more immigrants stream into America, this has become a ticklish issue. Schwarzenegger for his part will probably not see a first-generation naturalized American citizen as president in his lifetime. More than two dozen proposed constitutional amendments have been introduced in Congress to relax the restriction of natural-born citizen. Two of the more well-known were introduced by Representative Jonathan Brewster Bingham in 1974, with the intent to allow German-born Secretary of State Henry Kissinger (otherwise fourth in the line of succession to the presidency) to become eligible, and the Equal Opportunity to Govern Amendment by Senator Orrin Hatch in 2003, intending to allow eligibility for Austrian-born Arnold Schwarzenegger. The Bingham amendment would have also made clear the eligibility of those born abroad to U.S. parents, while the Hatch one would have allowed those who have been naturalized citizens for 20 years to be eligible. Bear in mind that all of these proposed constitutional amendments did not get past Congress, and even if they had, they would have to be ratified by the states to come into effect.

As presidential prospects, both Obama and Harris have broken the glass ceiling for second-generation American citizens, but not for first-generation immigrants. (When I say first-generation, I mean foreign born; second-generation means native-born.) Also, there is the loophole of the dual citizenship as discussed earlier.

Is America ready for a foreign-born citizen to become president? I would hazard no. Already many people in the country, white and black and even Hispanic, are seething against immigrants. If California Republic (as the state is formally called) were a separate country, maybe. About thirty years ago, the white population of the state dipped to less than 50% of the state's overall population. Today it stands at 35%. Latinos are 40% and seem to be ever-growing. California is the first state in the nation with an immigrant man in Arnold Schwarzenegger as governor. Perhaps if California was a separate nation, it would amend its laws to have someone like Schwarzenegger as its president.

But not the rest of the country. Not yet. Perhaps in 50 years. A foreign-born person would have to display his undivided loyalty to America. How can one prove that? He would probably have to be Christian. And his American accent would have to be flawless, meaning he could not get by with an alien-sounding drawl. He would probably have had to have served in the US military. Americans are a very nationalist people, and I mean nationalist here in a good sense, in a super-patriotic way. They are not going to hand the keys of the Ferrari to someone they don't trust. The same goes for the nuclear codes. Even though California is the bellwether state of the union, the rest of the country considers it whacko. Believe me, I have lived in every part of the country, from Texas to California to the Midwest to the Deep South with sojourns in between in New York and the Pacific Northwest. Much of the US is highly conservative and protective of the Constitution as it is. The Constitution is revered in the US. It would be impossible in current climes to have it amended to accommodate a foreign-born president. Never say never, but not ready is the answer for now.

If the level of immigration keeps up, it becomes even more impossible because native resentment against foreigners builds up. If immigration is halted, at least for 20-25 years, then maybe the country would grow more accepting of foreigners than it already is (I would like to emphasize here that America is fairly tolerant of foreigners; it's just that resentment against them is increasing). Nativity is no surety of allegiance or loyalty, but jus soli (right of the soil, meaning birthright citizenship) and birth to a US citizen even if present overseas, are all we now have to determine allegiance and loyalty.

I'll give you my example. I am 55. I have lived in the US 28 years, almost all my adult life. I came to the US at 21, at a very impressionable age, barely out of my teens. I have foregone my Indian citizenship for the American. Yet in America, I am always seen as Indian. Because I am perceived as Indian there, I feel Indian there. In India, I don't feel Indian. I feel American even though people in India perceive me as Indian based on how I look. I am a real nowhere man. I am not patriotic to any country. I am a schizophrenic personality. Should I be president of the US? Absolutely not. Should I be prime minister of India? Equally absolutely not. My lived experiences have made me who I am. If I had not come to America, I would have remained Indian heart and soul.

I still cheer the Indian cricket team, sometimes. I have been in India two years. I find India anarchic. I miss the order of the US and the straightforwardness of its people. I will probably move back to the US, hopefully sooner than later. I am only giving my example to denote how complex being an immigrant is. Kamala Harris cannot claim to be Indian or Jamaican in any serious setting in the US just as Barrack Obama cannot claim to be Kenyan. They are first and foremost, and only, Americans. That's why they have gotten the chance to become US president. Any split personality like me, no, no, no. Now another foreign-born immigrant might come along and say that I am totally devoted to America. Then prove it. That's the challenge for a foreign-born citizen to become president of the United States of America. In a fight with his native land, where will the foreign-born US citizen's unalloyed loyalty lie, with the US or with his native land? Having a foreign-born US citizen as president is complicated to say the least.

Note that John McCain, Ted Cruz, and Tulsi Gabbard all had varying circumstances but none were born in the US, but all of whom were allowed to make a run for the presidency, with McCain, in 2008, coming closest to the Oval Office when he won the Republican nomination for the presidency, but who was eventually defeated by Barack

Obama in the general election. It seems that the definition of natural-born citizen is that you are either born in the US, or you can be born overseas but to at least one parent who is a US citizen. That's how McCain, Cruz, and Gabbard got through. Despite not being born in the US, they were born to an American parent. That also means that the "birther" conspiracy launched by Donald Trump against Barack Obama, that the latter was not born in the US and therefore ineligible to be president was fundamentally flawed because even if Obama had been born in Kenya as Trump asserted, he would have been born to a mother who was a US citizen and therefore a natural-born citizen qualified to be president.

Also note that as per a 2016 **CBS News** poll, only 21% of Americans would favor changing the Constitution to allow people who are not natural-born U.S. citizens to become president, while 75% would oppose such a change. So it's highly unlikely that anything will change in this regard in the near future.

8. The Third World must rectify itself

The world is divided into three worlds—the First World, which includes America, Canada, northern and western European countries, and Japan. The Second World was the former Warsaw Pact bloc, but now means Russia and neighboring countries like Belarus and Ukraine. The Third World comprises much of Asia and most of Africa. Most of the migration in population is from the Third World to the First World. Resentment against this migration is ever-growing in the First World, often becoming violent and taking the shape of race riots instigated by natives against the migrants, as has been happening these days (August 2024) in the UK.

Nobody wants lives lost and property damage. But such is the effect of mass migration from the Third World to the First World. Anger in the First World is at a boiling point. Even if many natives do not become violent, subliminally they are against immigration and feel that enough is enough. Let's consider the case of India, a prominent Third World country that is the biggest country in the world in terms of population (1.4 billion) and that sends lots of migrants to the First World, and even a small amount to the Second World.

India today is the fifth largest economy in the world (approx. $4 trillion), but fares poorly in the United Nations Development Programme (UNDP)'s Human Development Index (HDI). The HDI is a summary measure of average achievement in key dimensions of human development: a long and healthy life, being knowledgeable and having a decent standard of living. The HDI was created to emphasize that people and their capabilities should be the ultimate criteria for assessing the development of a country, not economic growth alone.

The HDI is broken into human development groups: very high human development, high human development, medium human development, and low human development. For 2022, Switzerland ranked no. 1 with an HDI of 0.967. The US, even though it was in the very high development group, ranked 20, with an HDI of 0.927. India came in at 134, in the medium development group, with an HDI of 0.644. In contrast, Pakistan came in the low development group with a rank of 164 and an HDI of 0.540. In total, 193 countries were ranked.

India's case is unique. It's a flourishing democracy, yet it has not been able to significantly improve the lot of its people since independence from the British in 1947. Note that Algeria comes in the high development group with a rank of 93 and an HDI of 0.745. Despite its many achievements, what has India done wrong? Jawaharlal Nehru was India's prime minister from 1947-64, a full seventeen years. He is regarded as the maker of modern India. He built dams, roads, bridges, the power grid, India's renowned space program as well as its nuclear program, India's famous engineering schools (the Indian Institutes of Technology), India's business schools (the Indian Institutes of Management), etc. He was personally incorruptible.

So was the freedom-fighter generation that led India right after Independence. They were honest and imbued with a sense of service. At the time of Independence, India had a population of roughly 350 million. Nehru never saw population growth as a problem and took no steps to curb it. India's population exploded. From 1975-77, the regime of prime minister Indira Gandhi tried harsh measures such as mass vasectomies to curb the population explosion, but the effort rebounded on her. The people couldn't tolerate the harsh measures and threw her out of power. The whole population control movement was led by her rogue younger son, Sanjay.

Sanjay's evil-doings led to family planning becoming a hot political potato in India. No Indian prime minister since 1977 even talks about controlling the population, leave alone taking steps to slow down the population explosion. Narendra Modi is India's current prime minister. He became PM in 2014. In his first independence day speech given from the ramparts of Delhi's Red Fort in 2014, he stressed the need to control India's population. He said that all the gains India makes economically and otherwise are overrun by the exploding population. But this was just lip service at best. Modi has given nine other independence day speeches from the Red Fort. Not once again has he brought up the subject of India's population. His advisors must have heeded him so. They must have told him touching the subject of population was like bringing the kiss of political death on oneself.

Marriage and babies are central to Indian life. Look at all the serials on Indian TV. They are all about marriage and having babies. This propensity cuts across all classes, the rich and the poor alike, and every religion. I was talking to a friend. She recited me a short story. An Indian and a Chinese were talking to each other. The Chinese asked the Indian, what do you want from China? The Indian replied, infrastructure, infrastructure, infrastructure. The Indian in return asked the Chinese, what do you want from India? The Chinese replied babies, babies, babies. China's one-child policy has helped shrink its population. Many Chinese women don't want to have babies. China's population too is 1.4 billion (actually 1.409 billion whereas India's is 1.417 billion), but is tapering off while India's is growing at a rapid clip. No wonder the Chinese government has rescinded its one-child policy and encourages its population to breed.

The Chinese National Bureau of Statistics said the total number of people in China dropped by 2.08 million, or 0.15%, to 1.409 billion in 2023. That was well above the population decline of 850,000 in 2022, which had been the first since 1961 during the Great Famine of the Mao Zedong era. India's population is growing year over year at 0.7% and the US's population is growing year over year at 0.4%. The Chinese economic miracle has made the country leap into the high development group with a rank of 75 with an HDI index of 0.788. Even though, like India, China sends bucket loads of students to study in the West, one does not hear of much illegal migration from China as one hears from India.

Unabated population growth is only one reason that India is lagging behind. Endemic corruption is another. India has had fourteen prime ministers since 1947. Most of them were good men and women, personally honest, and dedicated to building the country. It was not until the rule of Indira Gandhi, daughter of Nehru, which started in 1966 that corruption started taking hold in India. Gandhi was seen to be personally incorruptible, although her opposition called her the fountainhead of corruption. It was true that she allowed her party, the Congress, to rake in the moolah. In days gone by, party canvassers used to go from door to door and raise small amount of money from donors. This money was called *chanda* and went into the party fund to fight elections and for other necessities. Sanjay changed all that. He noticed that India was importing large defense systems from overseas. He decided that he would buy these arms only if his party received a significant kickback. No longer was there any need for the painful *chanda*

collection. The party was flush with kickbacks.

India's defense needs only grew—India fought a war against China in 1962, and two

against Pakistan, in 1965 and 1971—so the amount of kickbacks grew concomitantly.

Opposition parties could only watch with envy as the Congress grew richer and richer.

Since the kickbacks had the blessings of Gandhi, ordinary people took it upon themselves

to engage in bribery without the fear of getting caught. Slowly but surely, all sections of

society, including the police and the judiciary, became corroded.

India does not have much oil, but it is blessed with other resources—iron ore, bauxite and

other minerals. In order to do business, one had to adhere to a new *license permit quota*

raj. The government would have its hands in every till. It would give licenses and permits

to do business to favored industrialists under a system of quotas. The industrialists would

then give kickbacks to chosen government functionaries. India's politicians came from

mostly humble backgrounds. It was the elite Indian Administrative Service (IAS) that ran

the show.

During the British Raj, the Indian Civil Service (ICS) comprised mostly of Britishers

served as the steel frame of the empire. The officers were inscrutably honest, but lived

like lords. When the British left India, the IAS came into being. Its purpose was the same

as the ICS. But after Nehru died, slowly but surely, the IAS became corrupt. In the Indian

state of Bihar, where being from the IAS is very prized, a male officer can command

dowry in the millions of dollars. His father-in-law knows that his son-in-law would help

him recover ten times his investment.

India's politicians come under flak for sleaze, and so should they be, but they keep rotating. One political party comes into power, and then goes into the wilderness, while another party comes in. Many of the politicians are not savvy enough to indulge in large-scale corruption while keeping their hands clean. An IAS officer is a permanent fixture. She has seen how to cheat and bribe and loot in every administration. She is the one who teaches the politician assigned to her how to become a scumbag. In the process, she takes her own hefty cut.

Corruption has grown like a cancer in India, spreading its tentacles to every corner of government and society. As India grew economically, a healthy middle class developed. The powers that be decided that they would not focus on exports; instead the domestic market provided captive consumption. The industrialists were delighted. They would not have to strive to make world-class products but could make do with shoddy products purely for domestic consumption as long as they bribed the government, the politicians as well as the bureaucrats. Corruption has ensnared India like the tentacles of an octopus. Go to buy a railway ticket. Pay the government clerk a bribe. Go to collect a parcel from the post office. Pay the government clerk a cut. Corruption has grown like a cancer even at home. The domestic help gets its monthly salary, but to get them to do any job properly, you have to bribe them constantly. An American Midwestern work ethic is missing in India.

The weather—hot and sultry—nine months in a year too makes people lazy and languorous. I asked my father why India doesn't progress as fast as some other countries. He replied that basically Indians were a content people. A *chalta hai* (anything goes) attitude prevails. All of the aforementioned ills resulted in the country going bankrupt in

1991 and its gold reserves being hauled to the Bank of England in London. Indians would have to mend their ways.

Manmohan Singh became finance minister in 1991, and in one fell sweep dismantled the *license permit quota raj.* Now businesspeople would have to understand the Indian market and compete with one another. A ferocious entrepreneurial energy was unleashed. The government stopped hiring. Jobs were there only in the private sector. One could not laze about in a private sector job; one had to work. Better products and services, even if not up to world standards, started emerging in India.

But once gain the Indian devious mind took over. In 1991, there were zero dollar billionaires in India. As of April 2023, India had 167 dollar billionaires, number three in the world after the US and China. Crony capitalism on a large scale had taken over the earlier petty *license quota permit raj.* Dhirubhai Ambani, a famous industrialist, is said to have remarked that his only customer was the government. His son, Mukesh, is worth over a $100 billion today. Industrialists mined India's national resources and minted money. Want to become a steel magnate? Just pay the government a healthy cut and you will get access to the country's iron ore resources. Want to sell electricity, buy coal at dirt-cheap rates. Want to become the country's ports czar? Buy the government to give you contracts to build airports and seaports.

Manmohan Singh became prime minister in 2004, but his government dissolved in a miasma of sleaze and corruption in 2014. Though personally honest, he let matters slide so that there were multiple scams worth more than $40 billion in allocating telecom spectrum, coal, and other resources. There was a wave of anger in the country over corruption. Massive protests were held countrywide but nobody was really taken to task.

Whoever was found guilty was set free soon thereafter. One could be corrupt with complete impunity in India. Judges could be bribed. While nothing came out of the wave of protests, Narendra Modi rode the anger to become India's prime minister in 2014. Like Manmohan Singh, Modi is seen to be personally incorruptible, but he has allowed crony capitalism to flourish. On top of the list of crony capitalists is Gautam Adani, who too is worth over $100 billion. Then comes Mukesh Ambani, and then sundry others. Adani and Ambani pay for Modi's election expenses. In return, he rewards them with fat and juicy contracts.

Because of such sleaze and palm greasing, there is not a single world-class product to India's name. India is famous for its software engineers. India exported nearly $200 billion of IT software and services in 2023, but even in that space, India has yet to come up with a branded software product that is a household name in the West. Perhaps India's most renowned export product is the Indian Institute of Technology engineer.

What India has done well is expand its middle-class and upper-class to about 400 million. That still leaves 1 billion of the population, 600 million of which exist on less than $2 a day. In the general election of 2024, the opposition claimed that 700 million people in India, especially in the rural areas, were unemployed and the government had no answer to that. The 400-million middle- and upper-class is both a blessing and a curse. Blessing because there is a huge market for providers to cater to. A curse because we are in the same place as we were before the *license-permit-quota-raj* was dismantled. The market is captive, although competition now is much greater than before and choices before consumers are vast.

Until 1991, there were only three cars an Indian could buy: an old version of Fiat, a version of the Morris Minor called the Ambassador, and Maruti-Suzuki, a car that the Japanese corporation, Suzuki, was making in India. Today, almost every car manufacturer is selling in India. Tesla is poised to enter India to make its electric cars.

There are two ways that an Indian can buy a foreign-branded car in India. One is to import directly from abroad, pay the relevant duties, and take the car home. The other is buying a foreign car made in India. For example, both Mercedes and BMW are making in India. To make a foreign car in India, the government of India laid down the rule that 80% of the car's components must be sourced from Indian manufacturers.

Is this happening? No. Foreign car manufacturers bring in their cars in semi-knocked down condition to their manufacturing plants in India, which are really assembly plants, assemble the cars, and paint and polish them in India. If they source any components from Indian vendors, these are non-essential components. How are foreign car makers skirting Indian laws?

It is with the connivance of the Indian government. The car manufacturers pay bribes to federal and state governments to essentially sell a foreign-made car in India. The Indian government is only too happy to have its own 80% Indian vendor rule be violated with impunity. Indian consumers are happy too. They would much rather have a German-made car than a car with a German brand but with 80% Indian components. They trust German components and engineering much more than they trust Indian components and engineering. So everybody is happy—the foreign car manufacturer, the Indian government, and the Indian consumer—and life goes on merrily. India today is flooded with every conceivable car, from top-of-the-line brands to economy models.

Corruption has seeped into every vein of the Indian body politic. The 400-million middle- and upper-class is both ravenous for goods and services and rapacious in the intensity with which they consume without letting benefits trickle down to the lower classes. The trickle-down theory of economics, that money will flow from the top classes to the bottom classes, hasn't worked in India. Sure the middle- and upper-class is growing, but the dismally and desperately poor are growing even faster. All of the gains that the country makes get negated. India hosted the G20 summit in 2023. The G20 comprises the world's top 20 economies, amongst which are many developing states. India portrayed itself as having arrived on the world's economic stage with the world's fifth largest economy but its GNI (Gross National Income) per capita was the lowest in the G20. On the basis of 2017 PPP (purchasing power parity) $, India's GNI per capita is $6,951. China's is nearly three times more at $18,025.

In China, they lop off heads of government officials caught in corruption. India is not a communist dictatorship like China, so people will not brook head-lopping. In India, hardly any politician or bureaucrat get caught with their hands in the till, even though the vast majority has its hand in the till. An odd minister is ever sent to jail, but even there they have a five-star life, playing badminton and eating special meals brought from home and living in air-conditioned spaces. A male minister and a female minister belonged to the same party. The man would frequently make advances on the woman, which she would firmly repudiate. Both got caught in the same scam and were sent to the same jail. There they apparently kissed and made up, and now, out in the world, are on good terms.

 India aspires to be a First World country by 2047, a hundred years after independence from the British. Actually the target set in the nineties was 2020, but that year came and went without a whimper, so the goalpost was moved to 2047. What the government needs to realize that all the resources of the country cannot be gobbled by the 400 million middle- and upper-class, and one conveniently forgets the 600 million dismally and desperately poor. Foreign countries cozy up to the Indian government to tap into these 400 million people. India is also one of the biggest arms importers in the world, around $10 billion a year. It is common for arms deals to have kickbacks. So, again, foreign governments coddle up to India. India is like a gold rush for them. They are in no mood to call out the Indian government to get its act together. They are completely happy with the way things are in India.

It seems that the Mughal era is back in India, when the *amirs* (nobles) and some others like traders were super-rich and the rest of the country wallowed in poverty. All the European explorers of India—the British, the Dutch, the French, the Portuguese—were attracted by the wealth of the Indian nobility and that's why they came to India. A Mughal-era portrait shows the seventeenth century Mughal Emperor Jehangir taking aim with his bow and arrow at a black ghoul, which was meant to represent Indian poverty, but the situation today, four hundred years later, is still the same. Poverty is endemic in India.

Maybe the Indian government doesn't realize what it means to be a First World country. It is not just a question of economics alone. By 2047, India will be the world's third largest economy. But will it have the mindset to become a western country? Will it have the systems in place like universal health coverage, social security, a safety net for the poor, and the like. Would people be able to be taken at their word? Will contracts be followed in letter and spirit? Will religious strife come down? Will discrimination against the Muslim minority and the Dalit Hindu outcastes diminish? Will corruption spiral downwards? Will India become a meritocracy, attracting the best and the brightest from all over the world to come to its shores to study and work? Will rule of law and justice prevail? These are the hallmarks of a western First World country.

It is only twenty-three years to 2047. Less than a quarter of a century. My guess is that India will grow economically, but it will forget the aforementioned hallmarks of a western country along the way. How then can India hope to call itself a First World country? It might become some version of China, economically more prosperous but behind in so many First World ways.

No god will descend upon India and the rest of the Third World to cure themselves of their ills. India is at least doing better than may other Third World countries, including its neighbor, Pakistan. There a military junta has been ruling pretty much since it was carved out of India in 1947. Pakistani military officers behave like *nawabs* (nabobs). They rule their country with an iron fist. Not only do they direct conventional army operations like securing borders but they are into all kinds of businesses like selling diapers, cereals, vegetables, etc. and constructing roads and highways. Whenever whim and fancy comes to them, they topple the civilian government and imprison civilian politicians. The civilians are called "bloody civilians" by them and are anyway serve as a veneer for military rule.

A country like Pakistan and many others in the Third World have to go ways before they aspire to be even India. They have many more ills than India. India is at least a functioning democracy with a relatively free press. Once again, Pakistan and the rest of the Third World will not set themselves right by themselves. But no alien from outer space will come to set them right either.

Speaking of aliens, Third World denizens are more than happy to become aliens in western countries. And their governments actually encourage them to do so. There are boat mafias in many Third World countries—from India and Pakistan to Algeria and Somalia—that haul people over the high seas—in particular the Mediterranean Sea which is hardly Mediterranean in nature, in fact it's treacherous—for a certain fee to the shores of Italy and Greece from where they make it to inland Europe. The trek is treacherous—ever so often one hears of fishing trawlers and dinghies capsizing with if not hundreds than tens lost at sea. The welcome in Italy and Greece for the migrants is to put it politely, not so welcoming. The Third World governments have within their power to break up these boat mafias, but they let them ply their trade regardless.

Other than immediate families, not a tear is shed for the dead migrants. Aside from an estimated statistic of the dead in papers and on web sites, nothing is known about them. Their lives are so worthless, in fact so condemnable, that even the names of dead and missing are not released to the public. The truth is no one wants to know. They become a matter of shame for their home countries. Across the world too, on land this time, not much is different. Reports have it that any number of Indians are being caught together with Mexicans and Central Americans trying to sneak into the US from Mexico. The Indians fly all the way to Mexico from where they begin their land journey to the US. They are treated horrendously by the US Border Patrol but they are desperate to make it to the promised land. Every Indian in the US who made it to the US surreptitiously has their own unique story of how they made it there.

Japan and Germany could lift themselves from the embers of World War II, albeit with US help, and become First World countries with almost negligible poverty. The US included Germany in its Marshall Plan. Would a Marshall Plan like-aid plan benefit India and Pakistan? I would hazard in the negative. Pakistan owes the International Monetary Fund (IMF) tens of billions of dollars. Pakistan's external debt is close to $150 billion. Yet the money that the IMF and other donors pour into Pakistan makes no visible impact on poor people's lives. Much of the money is gobbled up by the ruling elites. Countries like India and Pakistan believe in the messiah theory of development—that one day a messiah will arrive and cure their countries of corruption and poverty. That never happens. Even if a leader starts off well, he gets slowly tainted by corruption. The tolerance for corruption in these countries is infinite, so no leader can afford to dole out appropriate justice for corruption. Much of the money that Pakistan receives from the West goes in the ruling elite buying property in Dubai, London, and Toronto.

So what is the solution? The solution is exactly as leaders in India propose it. Paint a mirage 25 years hence, get everybody excited for a while, but as that mirage nears, stop talking about it and paint another mirage another 25 years later. Getting rid of their poor through boat and land mafias is one way Third World countries are tackling their population problems. Any poor person who comes in the clutches of the mafias and wants to leave the country is willingly allowed to leave the country. In fact, the governments are in on this trade, with government officials getting a cut from the mafias. How valiantly a man or a woman might have tried to save themselves and others at sea doesn't matter. What matters is that these are the poor, huddled masses—literally—who no one wants to care about. If they make it to the West, they become an invisible, estimated statistic that no one wants to count really.

One way of reducing your population growth is sending people en masse across land and sea namelessly to the West. The other is the more legal route. Whenever the Indian prime minister goes to an advanced country, he pitches for more jobs and educational visas for his county. Right now, the India-UK Free Trade Agreement is frozen over the question of how many Indians the British will allow in to their country. As I write this in August 2024, race riots are sweeping the UK with white hoodlums battering and beating the police and setting buildings on fire so that they can get their dirty hands on Third World Muslim immigrants. The UK is on a powder keg. Will the new Labour government of Keir Starmer be able to the manage the rioting is the million-pound question?

The US embassy in Delhi proudly reported that in 2022, over 1.2 million Indians visited the United States. Indians now represent over 10% of all US visa applicants worldwide, including 20% of all student visa applicants and 65% of all employment visa applicants. The US embassy and consulates in India have issued 1.4 million nonimmigrant visas in 2003, well surpassing the number in 2022. The US embassy in Delhi says that it welcomes this growth. Many of the student visas are not really nonimmigrant, with most Indian students staying back in the US to work. Even those going for employment, they try to do their best to get a green card. So other than tourists, some of whom also disappear into the US, these nonimmigrant visas are really immigrant visas. Let no one be fooled.

So exporting your best and brightest to the West is also no solution to your population woes. In 2023, India must have sent over a million people permanently to the West.

That's a pittance compared to its overall population of 1.4 billion. The Third Word must reduce its population, curb systemic and endemic corruption, manage its resources better, spend less on arms and more on development, if it has any hope of catching the First World. China showed the way, even if through draconian measures like the one-child policy and lopping off corrupt heads (at least those deemed corrupt). It also has not engaged in a war for nearly 50 years. (The last war that China fought was the Sino-Vietnamese War that lasted about a month in 1979.) Now China is near the top of the high development countries in the Human Development Index, waiting to break through into the very high development countries.

It's no one argument that the Third World ape China's brutal methods. So Third World countries like India, who want to enter into the First World club, will constantly find themselves on a treadmill to nowhere. They can't cure their ills, so they are stuck. Some percentage of their population will prosper, but the chasm between the rich and the poor shall ever increase. Those in the First World who believe that a country like India or Indonesia will develop fast enough to shortly knock on their doors for entry are deluding themselves. Nothing of the sort is going to happen.

9. What will the world look like in 2075?

The world's population in 2024 was 8 billion. In 50 years, by 2,075, it is slated to cross 10 billion. The population of the EU is 450 million, North America (excl. Mexico) 385 million, and of Oceania 45 million. The population of the First World therefore is 880 million.

The year over year growth in population in Europe is practically zero. So we can expect that that EU's population in 2075 will be 450 million. Net migration to the EU in 2024 was 1.6 million. Assume that every year there are 1.6 million migrants. Over 50 years, this would become 80 million additional migrants. As of 2023, 40 million residents in the EU were born outside the EU. So today we have a percentage of migration to be about 9%. In 2024, the migration would be (40 + 80) = 120 million migrants. Then the percentage of migrants in the overall EU society will be 37%, a four-time jump from today. No wonder alarm bells are ringing in the EU. The situation in North America will be almost as tense.

The year over year growth in population in North America is 0.6%. We can therefore expect NA's population in 2075 to be 520 million. The number of migrants in NA in 2024 was 1.7 million. Assume that every year there are 1.7 million new migrants. Additional migrants over 50 years would then be 85 million. As of 2023, 14% of NA's residents were born outside NA. Therefore, existing migrants are 54 million, and in 2024, the migrants would be (54 + 85) = approx. 140 million. As a percentage of overall population in 2075, that would be 36%, almost the same as that found in the EU.

Now, let's consider Oceania (Australia and New Zealand). Year over year growth in population is 1.2%. Expect then the population in 2075 to be 82 million. Each year from

2024, 140,000 migrants are added. So by 2075, there will be an additional 7 million migrants. Migration to Oceania is 29% of its overall population of 45 million, which comes to 13 million. So overall migration to Oceania = 13 + 7 = 20 million, or 24% of its overall population in 2075.

The situation then in the EU and in North America is dire. Assume that 40% of migrants die in in the next 50 years, that means in the EU 70 million migrants live, which is 14% of the populations of the EU. In NA, 57 million migrants, or foreigners born outside the shores of NA, live, which is also 14% of NA's overall population.

Migrants will breed. Assuming two migrants breed three children (taking into account grandchildren as well), the amount of the colored immigration population in the EU in 2075 will be 70 + (60 x 3) = 250 million, or 56%, well over half of the overall population. This is alarming for the EU's indigenous population.

In North America in 2075, 57 + (70 x 3) = 267 million, or 70% of the overall population of NA. NA's figures are even more startling than the EU's.

We are seeing an absolute colorization of North America and the EU. This is not meant to be a racist statement; it's just a statement of fact.

What if the migrants contribute to the building of the First World, as it was built by whites earlier, or even better than the whites, given the looming threats posed by China and India? Will all be hunky-dory then? Absolutely not. Europeans see themselves as the indigenous people of the EU. They don't want to be replaced by coloreds, or even by whites from other nations. For example, France would not like to be overrun by the Germans or the British, and the same can be said of any EU country. They want to maintain their skin color, but also their culture and language. Many Poles entered the UK as construction workers. That is one of the reasons that the British decided to do a Brexit. What happens if most of the migrants bring bad practices with them, which cannot be rectified when they reach the First World? For example, you may have a migrant from Central America who speaks no English and can only dig ditches. How many dig-ditchers does the US need? Can this dig-ditcher be transformed into a construction worker? That begs the question, how many construction workers does the US need? At a time when China and India are churning out research scientists, doctors, and MBAs, the US will be choc-a-block with uneducated migrants with rudimentary skills. How will they maintain America's greatness and past glories? It would be impossible. America will slide into Third Worldliness.

Just remove your rose-tinted glasses for a second. The great replacement theory, or white extinction anxiety, are starkly in-your-face, justified by numbers. Many people feel that what is happening is divine justice for white Americans. Didn't their forebears settle the land and move Native Americans away from it? That may be true, but it's also true that whichever people conquer a land don't give it back so easily. Immigration is a silent genocide for white people in North America, the EU, and Oceania. Their traditional habitats are being disturbed.

Most of the inventions and discoveries of the world have been made by people of the First World. As the rich empires of India, Turkey, and Persia slept, people in Europe had their Renaissance as well as the Age of Enlightenment. In the opening ceremony of the Paris Olympics of 2024, the Last Supper was mocked. Jesus himself was made a mockery of. Some people didn't bat an eyelid; most others took it in their stride. Nobody died. Imagine if the holy figures of Islam had been so mocked.

Europe and North America have self-reflected for centuries altogether and come out of the dark ages. They have put religion where religion should stand, as a personal matter. Many migrants are of an opposing disposition. Religion guides their lives. When they will become numerous in Europe and North America, they will make sure that their religion guides the lives of other people as well. They will send America and Europe to the dark ages, never to be rescued again.

Elon Musk claims that civil war is impending in Europe. That may or may not happen. Race riots though are a constant feature of the landscape. Just see what is happening in the UK today (as of August 2024). See how neo-Nazi thugs in Germany firebombed Syrian asylum shelters in 2015-16. Will all this escalate into a civil war? And if there is civil war in Europe, there will be a civil war in the US for sure. North Americans are armed to the teeth, much more so than their brethren in Europe are.

The numbers are bleak, at least for the indigenous populations of North America and Europe. It's an uncomfortable truth, but it's the truth: at the current levels of migration, the great replacement theory is real, the white genocide theory is real, white extinction anxiety is real. In fact, after seeing these numbers, it should be called white extinction panic.

Let's just do the numbers when there is no new net migration to the EU or NA.

The EU has a population of 450 million in 2024, and will continue to have so in 2075. As of 2023, 40 million residents in the EU were born outside the EU. There will be no new net migration from 2024 onwards. Assuming that 50% of the migrants die in the next fifty years. That means by 2075, there will only remain about 4% first-generation migrants. These migrants will breed. So you will have 20 + (20 x 3) = 80 million mostly colored immigrants in the EU, which is about 18% of the population.

Let's see what happens in NA when you the math. NA's total population is 385 million in 2024. NA's population is expected to be 520 million in 2075. Additional migrants from 2024 onwards until 2075 were expected to be 85 million, which are not there, so the real population of NA in 2075 is (520 – 85) = 435 million. The number of migrants already in NA in 2024 was 54 million. Assuming that 50% of the existing migrants die in the next fifty years. That means by 2075, there will only be 5% first-generation migrants. Let's count the total number of immigrants. That will be 27 + (27 x 3) = 108 million, who will almost all be mostly colored, which will be 25% of the overall population.

This is not racist match. I didn't start off with a number in mind and then work backwards. I used publicly available reliable data and then worked my way forward. I am stunned at my findings, as I hope that you will be as well. The death rates in the first case, that of projected migration, and when zero new migration is taken into account are different. In the first case, new migrants will have a lower death toll because they tend to be younger than existing migrants, so the death toll until 2075 was considered at 40% of all first-generation migrants. In the second case, there are no new migrants. The existing migrants tend to be old and their death rate has been considered to be 50% of all first-generation migrants.

10. Is there a way out?

From my findings, the anger of those who believe in the great replacement theory or white extinction anxiety is real, even though their methods—race riots; fire bombing and arson of migrant shelters; migrant lynchings, shootings, and beatings—most definitely are not. Nor are racism and discrimination. The people you already have, even if from misplaced policies from the past, you treat gently as if they were your own. There is fear of miscegenation between races, especially between white women and colored migrants, but personal choices must be respected.

Even if you completely bring down the immigrant hatches in 2024, you still have a colored migrant population of 25% of the overall population in North America (excl. Mexico) in 2075 and in the EU of about 18%. The EU is problematic because space there compared to North America is limited and it is already very crowded. So the First World needs to stop all migration. But they don't want to. They want nurses from the Philippines and India. They don't want to train their own nurses. Their people want to be cared for but don't want to go into the medical care business. Nursing is still a prestigious job. More lowly jobs are even more shunned. Unskilled workers from the Third World must be called for all these road-laying, construction, agricultural and dig-ditching jobs. I lived in Texas for two years and never saw a white man doing any road construction. He was always the supervisor; Latinos were always the road layers.

The same unfortunately is true in the corporate sector. White people grab all the positions of power (there are exceptions of course) and then boss around over the Indians and the Chinese. I always felt that I was the one who came up with ideas, and my white boss ran with them. At some point I thought that my endless pool of ideas would run dry. I was in sales and marketing and not in engineering. In STEM (science, technology, engineering, math) areas, workplace theft is still fairly limited because whites who have gone into STEM areas tend to be intelligent. But many whites don't want to go into STEM subjects. They prefer the humanities. From what I have seen, many non-STEM whites party during their years in college and then decide to go into greyish areas like sales, marketing, and human relations.

Human relations has almost become the preserve of white women. So also secretarial jobs. Sales and marketing is one way to make it to the top of a company, so the competition is fierce. All's fair in business. If the colored immigrant even as much as demurs about workplace theft, racism or discrimination, he is hauled into HR and read the riot act and marginalized from company meetings. He has no choice but to leave the company. His prospects there were dim in any case, and they had become even dimmer, in fact non-existent after his complaint. Most Indians and Chinese keep their heads down. They were hired to be worker bees and they intend to stay that way. They don't want to return to their homelands. They are given a healthy salary, which pays for the needs of their families, and so they keep quiet and lump it.

There are only a few immigrants who retain the ambition to make to the top. I wanted to be CEO of a company by age 40. In part through job-hopping, I made it to the vice-president of a $5 billion company. It was there that I hit my glass ceiling and couldn't shatter it anymore. I left my area—the energy sector—to pursue a career in writing and journalism.

So, the First World wants immigrant STEM worker-bees because their populations are not going into STEM. Every once in a while, you will find hoardings on the road exhorting American students to go into STEM. American politicians do it all the time. Black Americans in particular spurn STEM. STEM has led to the American leadership of the world with companies such as Google, Apple, Amazon, Microsoft, and Facebook, as also with the companies that develop arms and ammunitions. So, First World politicians are addicted to world dominance and will continue to import brilliant STEM workers from the Third World.

Third World politicians too are content exporting STEM workers. They get healthy remittances from them. But how healthy are they? According to the Word Bank, in 2022, remittances to India topped $120 billion for the year. India is a $4 trillion economy. Remittance are just 3% of that. India today has an upper- and middle-class of 400 million. With its best and brightest leaving for the First World, the Indian economy, impolitic though it might be to say it, has been built mainly by its second-rate people. What if the best and brightest were forced to stay behind? Where would India go then? The best STEM engineers in India come from the acclaimed government-run heavily-subsidized Indian Institutes of Technology that provide education at a cost that is a pittance when compared to American standards, but which many believe provide a science and technology education better than even the top-ranked Massachusetts Institute of Technology. Very often one sees that in MIT or other elite American technical universities, the toppers are Indian followed by the Taiwanese. IIT students go through a grueling exam to gain admission. It is common that whichever student attains the top rank in the IIT entrance examination is made an offer to come and study at MIT instead on a full scholarship. Many IIT graduates go to graduate school in the US to study and stay. A Third World country like India is subsidizing the economy of a First World powerhouse like America.

The Singaporean government has found a way. I used to teach tech laboratory classes to students at the University of Illinois at Urbana-Champaign, USA. I had a few Singaporean students in my class. At the outset, I must say that they were brilliant. They told me that they were studying in the US on a full scholarship from the Singaporean government, but they had had to sign a bond with their government to return to Singapore and serve not just in the private sector, but in government service. See how Singapore has bloomed. Just see how a Third World country like Singapore prospers and joins the ranks of the First World when its best and brightest run the show. That is one possible solution for India and other Third World countries to build their economies. Even if the Indian government cannot afford an American education for every deserving student, it can tell each IIT admittee: see, we have provided you a top-class undergrad education at a cost that is laughable by American standards and a quality that is possibly even better than most American universities would provide. If you want to go to America for graduate study, you have to sign a bond to return to India after your graduate study to work in India for at least 10 years, otherwise we are not letting you into an IIT.

Such a proposition would raise a hullabaloo in India. But something has to be done. It is India that will benefit most from keeping its best and brightest, who today are lured by greener pastures in the West, without any penalty being imposed upon them. Just see where India goes by keeping its best and brightest. Its economy will skyrocket so much that its best and brightest will not want to leave the country.

Such a scenario American politicians do not want. They do not want India to come up to the level of America. They will keep paying lip service to stopping immigrants, while making sure that the best and the brightest of the Third World will make it to their shores. As I have discussed earlier, there is a crying need for unskilled Third World workers in the West. If an unskilled European or American decides not to take up a so-called menial job, that is, basically not to work, he can always lie on his couch and survive on government welfare. Such welfare is not available to uneducated Third World immigrants, so they are forced to do the dirty jobs.

The bottom line is that the West will try to curb some immigration, especially that of uneducated migrants, but that won't be enough. The browning of the Third World will go on relentlessly, which will further antagonize the West's indigenous people. And that antagonism is not confined to just the alt-right. It is prevalent everywhere. Elections show that. In America. In France. In the Netherlands. In Germany. Race riots are engulfing the UK. If the situation is so bad now, will it lead to civil war? Possibly. Hatches down to immigration of all kinds is the only solution, but will the powers that be in the West heed that? In America, Donald Trump is the anti-immigrant demagogue, in France it is Marine Le Pen, in Holland it is Geert Wilders, in Germany it is Alice Weidel. The list goes on. Some of them like Trump and Wilders have tasted power. Le Pen and Weidel, not yet. But it is only a matter of time before they do so. Shouldn't today's moderate western rulers blunt the appeal of the absolute racists like Trump and Wilders and Le Pen and Weidel by clamping down on immigration of all kinds? If the trump card of the demagogues—ban immigration—is taken away, few will vote for them. And today's moderate western rulers would benefit not only their countries but also the Third World.

Britain instituted its Rwanda policy, where unwanted immigrants to the UK were going to be packed off to Rwanda. The UK has already paid Rwanda $300 million and built some housing for unwanted immigrants there. Keir Starmer, the new UK prime minister, has scrapped that plan. Apparently, Rwanda has refused to reimburse the $300 million to the UK. But such plans don't work. Italy plans to send thousands of asylum seekers to Albania. But these plans won't work. An asylum seeker has risked his life and spent his last dollar, in many cases gone into debt, to escape hell and find haven in his promised land, a country in the West, and you are forcing him to a similar hell that he came from. Worse still, the new hell will be strange to him. He will resist. You will shoot. That's what this immigration debate has come down to. Violence, violence, violence. A world engulfed in violence. Perhaps Elon Musk is right. There will be war, civil war in not only Europe, but America and Oceania as well.

The truth, the dirty truth is immigration greases the skids of the First World. It turbocharges their economies, compared to what the economies would have been without immigration. But it comes with some drawbacks. First, it antagonizes indigenous people economically. They feel that their jobs are being taken away by immigrants, and there may be some truth to that. Second, it colorizes their countries. White is right, and therefore white should stay white. Third, the indigenous people will not say it aloud, but many of their people, especially the women, find dark skin irresistible. Many white males detest inter-racial miscegenation and the product of that—little Obamas—floating around browning their white world. It all boils down to skin color after all, doesn't it?

About the Author

Writing is in Sunil's genes. His father, Lt. Col. B.R. Sharan, was a prolific writer whose books include *Status of Indian Women: A Historical Perspective.*

Sunil grew up in a home where five languages were spoken: English, Hindi, French, Punjabi, and Urdu. He has also learned German. With a gift for language and literature, Sunil won numerous prizes in school and university for writing and debating. A yearlong stay in France helped make him fluent in French.

Sunil has attended four universities around the world: Purdue University at West Lafayette, Indiana; the University of Illinois at Urbana-Champaign; the Ecole Polytechnique in Paris; and the Birla Institute of Technology and Science in Pilani, India. He has two master's degrees, one in electrical engineering and the other in physics. At the Ecole Polytechnique, he pursued the Jean Monnet Program, which is considered the French version of the Rhodes scholarship. He has worked in the marketing departments of world-class companies including L'Oreal (in Paris), Dell (in Austin), and GE (in Atlanta). He was a prolific generator of marketing collateral and business proposals in these jobs, all of which honed his writing skills.

Sunil has published about 600 opinion and research articles on politics, geopolitics, society, economy, and the military in such publications as *The Washington Post, Fortune, Huffington Post, The New York Post,* Canada's *National Post, The Times of India, The Statesman of India, Dawn* (Pakistan), and many others.

David Brooks, noted columnist at *The New York Times*, cited the author's work in a September 2011 column entitled "Where the Jobs Aren't." *The New York Times* has also interviewed Sunil, as has *Al Jazeera*. *The Atlantic* magazine and the Aspen Institute have invited the author to speak at their annual conference, the Washington Ideas Forum, on how to reinvent the American dream. CNN, CNBC, and FOX have invited the author to their programs to talk about jobs and the economy.

The author's biography of the prime minister of India, Narendra Modi, has been published by Bloomsbury in 2021. The author's book on the Coronavirus pandemic has been published by RosettaBooks of New York in 2020. The author's latest book on how he came to Christ has been published by Wipf and Stock in 2021.